MUSIC BOX

Veronica Clark

Exploring music with young children

EDUCATION

About the author
Veronica Clark is the headteacher at Pashley Down Infant School in East Sussex. She is the author of two well-known music books for young children, *Music through topics* (Cambridge University Press, 1990) and *High low dolly pepper* (A & C Black, 1991).

Published by BBC Educational Publishing, a division of BBC Education, BBC White City, 201 Wood Lane, London W12 7TS

Designer: Jo Digby
Editor: Caroline White
Illustrator: Zoe Figg

First published 1995

ISBN 0 563 37315 6

Colour reproduction by Goodfellow and Egan, England
Printed and bound by Ebenezer Baylis & Son Ltd

CONTENTS

AUTUMN

Body language	10
Clothes	16
In the woods	20
Machines	25

SPRING

It's raining, it's pouring	54
Hens, chicks and eggs	59
Full of beans	64
In the kitchen	68

WINTER

Bedtime	32
Journey into space	38
Jingle bells	43
Getting around	47

SUMMER

Princes and princesses	76
Big bears and little bears	80
Frogs and ducks	84
Creepy crawlies	89

Introduction

Music Box is a music resource book for young children and their teachers. The themes of the sixteen units will be familiar to those who work in nurseries, playgroups and infant schools. Princesses, machines, teddy bears, eggs and space are all popular topics with young children.

The sixteen units are grouped under four season headings: **Autumn**, **Winter**, **Spring** and **Summer**. If you want, you can start in September with **Body language** and work through the topics in the order presented, finishing the year with **Creepy crawlies**. Alternatively, you can pick and choose to suit yourself. Some of the topics, **Jingle bells**, for example, are seasonal; others, such as **Machines**, can be covered at any time of the year.

The book contains a mixture of old and new, traditional and modern. Flick through the pages and you will come across lots of poems and songs which you chanted and sang as a child.

The structure of the units is simple. Each unit is in two parts: the first part contains poems, stories, chants and songs, which are accompanied by music teaching notes; the second part includes practical ideas for extending the unit topic into other areas of the curriculum. The five stamps below will help you to identitfy the elements within each unit:

| song | poem or story | rhyme | game | tape |

Musical skills

A wide range of musical skills are taught and practised in each unit. They include: singing, playing and clapping the beat; chanting and playing short rhythmic patterns; listening to and identifying changes in speed; producing realistic sound effects; making up short patterns of sound and recording them using symbols and pictures; reading simple scores.

The activities are easy to follow and easy to do. You don't need previous musical training to use this book. Just read the teaching notes, gather the children together and have a go. Don't expect to get it 'right' first time. Musical skills, like other skills, need to be practised. Repeat each activity two or three times – you will see and hear a marked improvement in the quality of performance. Encourage the children to listen carefully to what they are doing and you will get some amazing results!

Listening skills

Listening is the key to effective music-making. An audio cassette of songs taken from the BBC School Radio series *Music Box* is also available from BBC Educational Publishing (see Annual Order Form). The songs on the tape link up with the sixteen topics in the book (see page 7). They are lively, varied and full of exciting sounds. Each unit, under the heading **Music Box tape**, includes a suggestion for helping the children to focus their listening. When the children know the songs well, side 2 of the cassette provides the accompaniments to help you sing and play and maybe get ready for a performance.

Percussion instruments

Few of you will have access to a wide range of percussion instruments. It is recommended that schools, playgroups and nurseries have a small collection of good quality instruments supplemented by home-made sound-makers. The following collection of instruments is more than satisfactory for a group of approximately thirty children: two small tambourines, two small tambours (like a tambourine but without the jingles), two felt beaters, four hand jingles, two pairs of small maracas, four woodblocks, two rubber and four wooden beaters, two pairs of Indian bells (easier to play than triangles) and two guiros (or scrapers). Add to this collection of twenty instruments some home-made shakers, claves and stick jingles. Reduce the length of beaters which have long stick handles.

An octave of chime blocks (C D E F G A B C) with eight rubber beaters and/or a medium-sized xylophone (wooden bars) would be extremely useful. However, these items are expensive and you may decide to give a concert to raise money to buy them.

How this book works

A closer look at one of the units will give you a clearer picture of how this book works. Take **Journey into space**, for example.

The unit starts with the popular **story** *Whatever next!* by Jill Murphy. The teaching notes ask the children to make sound effects to accompany the telling of the story.

Making **sound effects** is a wonderful exercise for young children because it requires a lot of listening, discussion and practical music-making. First, the children focus on one of the sounds. What is it like: rough, smooth, tinkling? Is it loud or quiet? Does it get louder or quieter, or does it stay the same? What about the length of the sound? Does it go on for a long time or is it short? Is there just one sound or several? If there are lots of sounds, are they regular, like the ticks of a clock, or are they 'now and then'? Are they fast or slow?

Sound effects can be made with anything, including voices, parts of the body, musical instruments and other sound-makers (e.g. junk materials, furniture and play equipment).

In the story the children are asked to make the sound of Baby Bear's improvised rocket taking off. How can the children produce the right volume of sound? Is it possible to create an impression of a rocket rising in the air and disappearing into space? Outer space is a mysterious place. Can the children make a sound picture which evokes images of darkness, bright stars, meteors and the cold? The children are also asked to provide sound effects for the friendly owl, aeroplane, rain, landing and bath water.

The second activity focuses on an **action poem**, 'Five little astronauts'. It will take a few practices before the children know the poem well enough to join in with the teacher. Speaking together is a skill in itself. The children are then asked to play a descending run on a pitched instrument, followed by a splashing sound to describe the astronauts shuttling back to base. Here the children are practising their pitch recognition skills as well as using a combination of motor skills as they tap or rub bars and keys.

In **space chants** the children clap and play the rhythms of short space chants. They are also asked to relate the rhythms to printed symbols. This is the beginning of notation.

The final activity is a **song** called 'Spaceship to the moon'. It's fun, it's sung to a well-known tune, it has actions and it incorporates a vocal sound effect (Zooom!) and an increase in volume.

In the **listening section** the children are directed to listen to a song called 'I'm a green spaceman' on the *Music Box* tape.

The music section finishes with **more ideas** for singing, chanting and reading – still on the theme of space.

In the **cross-curricular links** section there are ideas for developing language work, maths, science, art and craft and drama.

Organising music sessions

How you organise your music sessions will depend on the time and space available and the age of the children. The youngest children in nurseries and playgroups may not be present every day, and this can create difficulties when introducing the more adventurous musical activities. However, the youngest children need the most practice, so don't be afraid to repeat the material several days on the run.

Most nurseries, playgroups and reception classes include short singing and chanting sessions as part of their daily routine. In addition to these, include a longer music session once or twice a week, but don't leave it to the end of the day when the children may be tired. These longer sessions are the times to introduce new material and to teach new skills. Begin and end with something familiar. The length of the session will depend on the age and experience of the children.

You must have good discipline for music sessions. Teach the children the rules and make sure they keep them, otherwise you will have noisy sessions, poor quality sound, spoilt instruments and frazzled nerves!

Sit on the floor in a circle or horseshoe. Some teachers choose to give each child a small cushion to sit on. Children who leave their place to play an instrument, dance or act can then easily find their way back – they simply look for their cushion. Put instruments and other sound-makers in the middle of the circle on a mat or on the carpet. Teach the children to handle them carefully. Can they pick them up and lay them down without a sound? Take instruments away from children who play them inappropriately, or who play at the wrong time. Xylophones and instruments with skins (e.g. tambourines, tambours and drums) should only be tapped with felt beaters. Save the wooden, rubber and plastic beaters for chime bars, woodblocks and glockenspiels.

Be prepared for your music sessions. Have an easel, paper and pens ready if you are including scoring activities, i.e. drawing pictures of sounds. Only put out the instruments you need. In any one session, concentrate on getting a few children to play a few instruments well. Massed instrumental playing is rarely satisfactory. Children can be involved in music-making without playing instruments – they can make body sounds, chant, sing and move. Work out your own system for ensuring that everyone has turns at playing the instruments.

On many occasions the children are directed towards the **music corner** to practise activities covered in class music sessions. There is no need to have a permanent music corner: set one up when the need arises. All you require is a table top, equipment as suggested in the teaching notes and a set of rules. Make it clear who is allowed to play in the music corner and for how long. Show an interest in what is going on there. Keep a record of who uses it. Encourage the other children to listen to music corner compositions. If you don't want the music corner to be used, cover it with a cloth.

Be calm in your presentation of music sessions. Move slowly and speak and sing quietly. Praise all effort. Encourage the children to improve their performance. They can only do this if they know what it is they are aiming for and if they listen carefully. Above all, have fun – because that's what music is all about!

Music Box tape
order and details of audio cassette

Body language
1 Head shoulders baby

Clothes
2 Poor nose

In the woods
3 Down in the forest

Machines
4 I'm walking like a robot

Bedtime
5 Get in the bath
6 Hushabye

Journey into space
7 I'm a green spaceman

Jingle bells
8 On Christmas Day

Getting around
9 Take you riding in my car

It's raining, it's pouring
10 Noah

Eggs and chicks
11 Old MacDonald had a farm

Full of beans
12 Our back garden

Big bears and little bears
13 Five big teddies

Frogs and ducks
14 Little green frog

Princes and princesses
15 There was a princess long ago

Creepy crawlies
16 Nine caterpillars

AUTUMN

My eyes can see

poem about parts of the body

My eyes can see,

My ears can hear,

My lips and tongue can talk;

My nose can smell,

My hands can clap,

My feet can run and walk.

Jan Betts

▶ Learn the poem and talk about the parts of the body. Which parts can make sounds?
Experiment freely with body sounds.

In the mirror

poem about noses

I looked in the mirror,
And looked at my nose.
It's the funniest thing
The way it grows:
Stuck right out there where all of it shows
With two little holes where the breathing goes.

I looked in the mirror
And saw in there,
The end of my chin
And the start of my hair.
And between, there isn't much space to spare
With my nose, like a handle, sticking there.

If ever you want
To giggle and shout,
And can't think of what
To do it about,
Just look in the mirror, and then, no doubt,
You'll see how funny *your* nose sticks out!

Elizabeth Fleming

▶ Sit in a circle and pass a mirror round. Ask the children to look at their noses.
Look for the holes 'where the breathing goes'. Hold your nose. Does it feel like a
handle? Wiggle your nose. Do you look funny?

I can see my nose, I can see my nose, I can see, yes I can see, I can see my nose.

I can see my nose

game song to the tune of 'The farmer's in his den'

I can see my nose,
I can see my nose,
I can see, yes I can see,
I can see my nose.

▶ What else can you see in the mirror? Make up some more verses to the song:

I can see my mouth . . .
I can see my ears . . .
I can see my hair . . .
I can see my eyes . . .

Out of sight

listening game based on body sounds

Rig up a screen for a child to hide behind (e.g. an up-ended table or a curtain draped over cane). Ask the child to make a sound with his or her hands, feet or mouth. Specify which part of the body is to be used. The rest of the children listen carefully and then copy the sound. Can they identify which part of the body made the sound? Can they describe the sound: loud, wobbly, long, up and down, high?

▶ Ask the child to come out from behind the screen and to repeat the sound so that the rest of the children can *see* how it was made.

▶ Choose someone else to go behind the screen and make a different body sound, and so on.

▶ When the children are familiar with the game, let *them* choose which part of the body to use to make the sound.

Who goes there?

sound discrimination game based on footsteps

This game is most effective if played in a room without carpet.

Sit the children in two rows facing one another. Leave space for a 'catwalk' in the middle. Ask a child with soft-soled shoes to march between the rows, from one end to the other. Listen to the footsteps. What do they sound like? Ask everyone to close their eyes and listen while the child walks back again.

▶ Ask a child with hard-soled shoes to do the same. Do the footsteps sound different? Ask the children to close their eyes and listen while he or she walks back between the rows.

▶ Listen to other foot sounds: bare feet, stockinged feet, high-heeled shoes, wellington boots, flippers, roller boots, clogs.

▶ Choose two contrasting footstep sounds. Listen to both of them at the same time. Can the children tell which is which with their eyes closed?

Hey Jim a-long

movement song

Hey Jim a-long, Jim a-long Josie.
Hey Jim a-long, Jim a-long Jo.

Walk Jim a-long . . .

March Jim a-long . . .

Skip Jim a-long . . .

Tip-toe a-long . . .

Jump Jim a-long . . .

▶ Encourage the children to match the movement to the words. Do not
expect them all to march, skip or jump in time with the singing – some
will, most won't!

Step in time

game to help children move in time with a beat or rhythm

Use a tambour to make a crisp marching beat. Ask the children to march
in time with the tambour like soldiers. Stop. Change to a faster, lighter
beat and ask them to run or jog around the room. Stop. Now pretend to
be giants, striding round the room to a slow, heavy beat. Try to match
strides to the beat of the instrument. Most younger children will need
lots of practice before they can to do this.

▶ Older children can try skipping in time to a rhythm. A skipping rhythm is
made up of long and short sounds. The words 'Half a pound of tuppenny rice'
have a skipping rhythm. Make the rhythm fairly fast; it is hard for children
to skip slowly.

▶ When the children have played the game several times, ask them to listen to the
tambour and decide for themselves which movement to make: march, run, stride
or skip. All except the skipping rhythm are regular and vary only in speed.

Down on the farm

animal sound game using voices

 Make a set of five to ten farm animal picture cards, including a tractor. Choose animals with distinctive sounds (e.g. pig, sheep, cockerel, horse, cow, mouse, cat, dog, hen). Show the cards to the children and practise making each sound in turn. Talk about the sounds. Are they high or low, short or long, loud or quiet? Find different ways to imitate them with voices.

▶ Sit four to six children in a circle. Put an animal card face down in front of each child. The starter turns his or her card over and says 'I went to the farm and I heard . . .' and instead of naming the animal, makes the sound. The next child repeats the phrase, includes the sound of the first animal, and then adds the sound of the animal shown on his or her card. Continue round the circle. The last child makes the sounds of all the farm animals.

▶ At the end of the game listen to all the animals making their sounds at the same time.

▶ Play the game with rainforest animals. Include a monkey, tiger, parrot, snake, elephant and crocodile.

Nursery rhymes

body and mouth sound effects

 Look out for opportunities to use body and mouth sound effects to illustrate well-known nursery rhymes and jingles: make a ticking sound with mouth clicks in 'Hickory dickory dock'; clap with cupped hands or thump chest or thighs to make the sound of galloping horses in 'The Grand Old Duke of York'; bleat like lambs before singing 'Mary had a little lamb'; ask three children to squeak during 'Three blind mice'; accompany 'This little piggy went to market' with grunts, adding a squeal at the end.

Music Box tape

listening and joining in

 **Head shoulders baby**
Listen to the song and touch the parts of the body as they are named. The tempo is lazy, so the children will have time to keep up with the singing. Ask a child to tap a tambourine quietly each time they hear 'One, two, three'.

More ideas

▶ Sing 'If you're happy and you know it clap your hands', 'We all claps hands together', 'Let everyone clap hands like me' and 'Everybody do this', which can be found in *Okki-tokki-unga* and *This little puffin* . . . Accompany the songs with a range of body sounds: tap knuckles, slice palms together, click fingers, slap thighs, tap and stamp feet, cough, whistle.

▶ There is a section on body sounds in *High low dolly pepper*.

Cross-curricular links

Language

▶ Learn the poem below. Add animal sounds.

Little piggy-wig

Little piggy-wig on the farm close by,
All by himself ran away from the sty.
The dog said 'woof',
The cow said 'moo',
The sheep said 'baa',
The dove said 'coo'.
Little piggy-wiggy began to cry,
And as fast as he could ran back to the sty.

▶ Write the four animal sounds on cards cut in the shape of speech bubbles:

▶ Make up mini 'Once upon a time' stories based on a body sound stimulus. Invite someone to make an interesting mouth or body sound, such as a hiss, and then make up a sentence about it: 'Once upon a time there was a long, long snake that liked eating mice.' Loud, slow thumps on the chest could lead to: 'Once upon a time there was a huge giant who stamped around in wellingtons.' The children will soon begin to offer stories of their own.

Maths

▶ Play counting games based on parts of the body. Start with one child and ask: 'How many eyes/feet/ears/noses has Sureya* got?'

▶ Establish that we have one nose, two ears, and so on. Make sets like below.

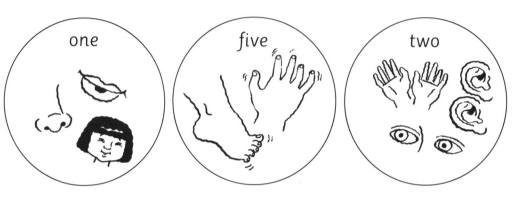

▶ Stand two or more children at the front and ask how many noses/eyes/fingers altogether.

▶ Play number echoes. Clap a number and ask someone to clap the same number back.

▶ Clap a number between one and ten, then ask someone to carry on clapping to ten.

▶ Make a see-saw with a plank and a pivot and use it to compare the weight of the children.

▶ Stand back to back and compare heights.

▶ Make surveys based on hair/eye/skin colour.

* substitute for name of child in group

Science

▶ Sing 'Head, shoulders, knees and toes' with actions. Check that the children can name these parts of the body.

▶ Draw round a child on a large sheet of paper. Paint on the hair, face, clothes, hands and feet. Cut out and label the head, arms, legs, hands and feet.

▶ Paint a large face. Cut out and label the eyes, hair, ears, mouth and nose.

▶ Talk about *same* and *different* in relation to skin colour, hair type, hair colour, height, shape and eye colour.

Art and craft

▶ Mix up a range of skin colours. Ask the children to find the colour closest to their own and to paint their face on a large card plate. When the paint is dry, add facial features and hair using paint, crayons, pastels, wool and buttons. Attach the faces to short lengths of dowelling and use them as masks. Swap over and pretend to be someone else.

Drama

▶ Tell the children that you are going to tell them what to do without talking. Ask them to look at you and then use hand and arm gestures to beckon, send away and wave hello, and to indicate that the children should sit down, fold arms, put hands on head, be quiet, and so on. Invite children to come to the front to give 'silent' instructions.

▶ Use body language to show anger, fear, sadness, happiness, excitement and shock. Don't forget facial expressions. Choose a well-known story, such as 'Little Red Riding Hood', to act out a range of emotions and situations. For example, the children jump up and down with joy when told that they can go and see Grandma. They skip happily through the woods, look frightened when they lose their way in the forest, act shocked as the wolf jumps out of bed, and cry when they discover that Grandma has been eaten. ●

The elves and the shoemaker

traditional story with sound effects

A shoemaker and his wife fall on hard times. No one visits the shop with orders for new shoes. The tools and leather lie gathering dust on the workbench.

One night, when the couple are asleep in bed, two elves slip into the shop and make a wonderful pair of shoes from scraps of leather which they find lying around. As the sun rises the elves slip away, leaving the shoes behind them.

The shoemaker can't believe his eyes when he finds the shoes. He has no trouble selling them and is able to buy some more leather.

The next night the elves come again. This time they make two pairs of shoes. This goes on for several days. Soon the shoemaker has queues of customers wanting to buy the beautifully made shoes.

He and his wife are able to buy food and clothes and their life becomes happy once more.

The shoemaker's wife is curious to find out who is making the shoes, so she and her husband hide in the workshop. As the clock strikes midnight the elves appear. They cut and stick and sew all night long. At sunrise they slip away under the door.

The shoemaker and his wife notice that the elves are wearing ragged clothes and have bare feet, and they decide to reward them for their kindness. They make warm trousers, coats, hats and tiny leather boots and leave them on the workbench. The elves are delighted with their new clothes. They put them on and dance around with joy. Then they slip away, never to return again. The shoemaker and his wife continue to enjoy good luck to the end of their days.

▶ Tell the story of the elves and the shoemaker. Read it from a book or make up your own version. The summary above may be helpful.

Sound effects

▶ Ask a child (the shoemaker) to make the sound of snipping and hammering using instruments (real or improvised): tap a beater on a book to make a hammering sound and scrape a guiro or comb for a snipping sound. Snip and hammer busily before the story begins, and then, as the narrator describes the misfortune of the shoemaker and his wife, slow down and, finally, stop. Keep silent for a few moments before continuing with the story.

▶ Choose an instrument to chime midnight. Point to a numberline to help the player count to twelve. Everyone can join in the chimes by chanting 'boing boing'. Keep the speed slow and the pace regular.

▶ Let the children experiment (one at a time) to find instrumental sounds to suggest magic. Play the magic music quietly and mysteriously each time the elves enter and leave the shop.

▶ Use the snipping and hammering sounds to describe the elves at work. Play quickly and quietly.

▶ Use the magic music to describe the elves dancing around in their new clothes. How might the instruments be played to suggest happiness?

Snip and tap

game based on two rhythmic patterns

Chant 'snip snip snip snip' over and over again, rhythmically and slowly. Make scissors with fingers and open and close them in time with the 'snips'. Briskly rub a guiro up and down in time with the chanting.

snip   snip   snip   snip

▶ Chant 'tip-per tap, tip-per tap' over and over again, rhythmically and slowly. Use fists for hammers. Choose instruments that make a tapping sound to accompany the chanting (e.g. woodblocks, claves).

tip - per   tap,   tip - per   tap

▶ Chant and play a pattern of snips and taps.

snip   snip   tip - per   tap,   snip   snip   tip - per   tap

▶ Make up and perform other snip-and-tap patterns.

▶ Put the two rhythms together. Begin with 'tip-per tap' and when the rhythm is well established add the 'snips'.

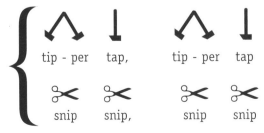

tip - per   tap,   tip - per   tap

snip   snip,   snip   snip

The elves' workshop

game for listening and co-operation

To play this game you will need a lot of clave-type instruments to represent tapping hammers. You will also need instruments that make rasping sounds for scissors. Cut up dowelling or broom handles for claves. Sandpaper or corrugated card stuck to blocks of wood make good rasps. Scrape with old pencils.

▶ Put the instruments on a tray and sit in a circle with legs crossed. Ask each child (elf) to take a tapping or scraping instrument from the tray. The children play their instruments in turn, either tapping (hammering) or scraping (cutting). When one child stops, the next child begins. They can play quietly or loudly, quickly or slowly, for a long or short time.

▶ Play the game cumulatively. Bring the children (elves) in one at a time by pointing to them. Once they have started they continue until everyone is busy. At a pre-arranged signal, everyone stops work. Alternatively, stop work one at a time.

All by myself

action song

I can put my shoes on, I can put my shoes on,
I can put my shoes on, all by myself.
All by myself, I'm a big girl/boy now,
I can do it, all by myself.

I can do my coat up, I can do my coat up,
I can do my coat up, all by myself.
All by myself, I'm a big girl/boy now,
I can do it, all by myself.

I can take my coat off . . .

I can do my zip up . . .

I can fasten buttons . . .

I can do my buckles . . .

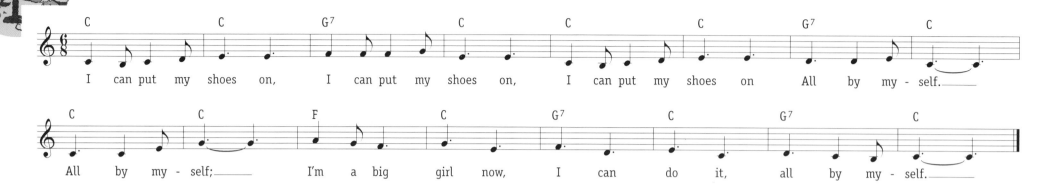

I can put my shoes on, I can put my shoes on, I can put my shoes on All by my - self.

All by my - self; I'm a big girl now, I can do it, all by my - self.

▶ Add some more verses to the song. Girls sing 'I'm a big girl now', boys sing 'I'm a big boy now'. Mime fastening buttons, taking off shoes, doing up zips, and so on.

Diddle diddle dumpling

rhyme for chanting and playing

x   x   x   x
Diddle diddle dumpling my son John,

x   x   x   x
Went to bed with his trousers on.

x   x   x   x
One shoe off and the other shoe on,

x   x   x   x
Diddle diddle dumpling my son John.

▶ Chant the rhyme all together, slapping or tapping a steady beat (see X above words, four per line). One child can play a quiet beat on a tambour.

▶ Draw or paint pictures of people wearing funny clothes in bed.

Music Box tape

listening and joining in

Poor nose

This song describes how hats and boots are worn in bad weather to keep heads and feet warm and dry. Nothing, however, is worn to protect the poor nose. Listen to the tape a few times until the song becomes familiar. Add simple actions. Tap your head slowly in verse one. Stomp from foot to foot in verse two. Hug yourself and shiver at each mention of wind, rain and sun. Rub your nose in the 'poor nose' chorus. Join in with the singing. Play maracas when the wind, rain and snow are mentioned. Clap or tap woodblocks on the word 'nose'.

More ideas

▶ Act out the story of the Emperor's new clothes.

▶ Chant 'John has great big wellington boots on' from *Knock at the door*.

▶ Read *Granny's quilt* by Penny Ives (Puffin, 1995).

Cross-curricular links

Language

▶ Make the play corner into a clothes shop. Include shoes, hats, scarves, gloves, bags and jewellery. If possible, provide safe mirrors. Let six to eight children dress up. Encourage the use of vocabulary of size (e.g. too small, too long, too tight).

▶ Play 'Who is it?' Describe the clothes of one child in the group. Whoever guesses the child's identity has the next go.

Maths

▶ Play games with pairs (e.g. socks, gloves, shoes). Mix up the items and then sort them into pairs. Count in twos. Talk about the odd one out. The children can colour and cut out a pair of paper gloves or socks, or they can colour one glove or sock and ask a friend to colour the other so that it looks the same.

Science

▶ On a warm breezy day wash the toys' clothes and hang them out to dry. Ask children to bring something in to wash. Which clothes dry the quickest? Why? Repeat the activity on a cold day.

Art and craft

▶ Rig up a long washing-line across the room. Ask each child to draw or paint a life-size article of clothing and decorate with lace, buttons, doilies and fabric. Cut out and hang on the line with pegs. Use the washing-line for language games and number work. For example, play I-spy or ask the children to touch: something that rhymes with 'beans'; something that you wear when it's cold; something that you wear on your feet. Ask how many things are on the line or what's next to the tights, and so on.

▶ Experiment with voices, instruments and other equipment to make the sound of the wind. Blow the washing to make it move.

▶ Sing 'David hang the stockings out' to the tune of 'Polly put the kettle on'. Act it out using the washing-line, pegs and paper clothes. Change the names and the clothing. At the end of the second verse make the sound of rain by tapping fingernails on the table or on a book.

> David hang the stockings out,
> David hang the stockings out,
> David hang the stockings out,
> The weather's fine.
>
> Rani get the stockings in,
> Rani get the stockings in,
> Rani get the stockings in,
> It looks like rain.

Drama

▶ Act out the story of the old man and the wind. The wind boasts that it is more powerful than the sun, and tries to prove it by blowing the coat off an old man. The man reacts by pulling his coat tightly around himself. Now it is the sun's turn. It shines gently down on the old man, who removes his coat. The moral is that you can't always get your way by using force. Find sounds to imitate the sound of the wind and the sun.

▶ Hold a fashion show. Make a corridor of chairs for the audience. The models can walk up and down between the chairs. Choose children to be commentators. Encourage descriptions of the clothes (e.g. colour, size, shape). ●

Little Rabbit Foo Foo

story song with actions and sound effects

(sung) Little Rabbit Foo Foo went hopping through the forest,
Scooping up the fieldmice and tapping them on the head.

(spoken) Down came the Good Fairy and said,

(sung) 'Little Rabbit Foo Foo, I don't like to see you
Scooping up the fieldmice and tapping them on the head.

(spoken) I'll give you three chances (CLAP CLAP CLAP)
After that, I'll turn you into a . . .*'

(sung) Little Rabbit Foo Foo went hopping through the forest,
Scooping up the fieldmice and tapping them on the head.

(spoken) Down came the Good Fairy and said,

(sung) 'Little Rabbit Foo Foo, I don't like to see you
Scooping up the fieldmice and tapping them on the head.

(spoken) I'll give you two chances (CLAP CLAP)
After that, I'll turn you into a . . .*'

(sung) Little Rabbit Foo Foo went hopping through the forest,
Scooping up the fieldmice and tapping them on the head.

(spoken) Down came the Good Fairy and said,

(sung) 'Little Rabbit Foo Foo, I don't like to see you
Scooping up the fieldmice and tapping them on the head.

(spoken) I'll give you one more chance (CLAP)
After that I'll turn you into a . . .*'

(sung) Little Rabbit Foo Foo went hopping through the forest,
Scooping up the fieldmice and tapping them on the head.

(spoken) Down came the Good Fairy and said,
'RIGHT, THAT'S IT!'
And she waved her magic wand round about her head
And turned him into a . . .*!

Lit - tle Rab - bit Foo Foo went hop - ping through the fo - rest, Scoo - ping up the field mice and tap-ping them on the head.

▶ Learn the song and add actions (see page 21). All the singing lines have the same
tune. The children will soon begin to join in with the Good Fairy's spoken lines,
becoming more angry as the drama unfolds. Shout the words 'RIGHT, THAT'S IT!'

* everyone makes a funny noise and pulls a funny face

Actions

LINE 1

Make two fingers into rabbit's ears and bounce your hand around in time with the music.

LINE 2

Make a scooping action with one hand, followed by a tap on the back of the other fist.

LINE 3

Make a descending flying action with both hands.

LINE 4

Wag your finger as though telling someone off.

LINE 5

As for line 2.

Sound effects

LINE 1

Tap a tambour or drum to suggest hopping – in time with the singing, if possible.

LINE 2

Make a scraping noise for the scooping (guiro) and a light tapping sound on a woodblock for the assault on the fieldmice.

LINE 3

For the arrival of the Good Fairy try a slide from high to low on a tuned instrument (e.g. glockenspiel, xylophone, keyboard).

LINE 5

As for line 2.

END OF SONG

For the magic at the end of the song make lots of quiet tinkling sounds (e.g. jingle bells, triangles, Indian bells, glockenspiels, chime bars).

Hop or fly?

listening game with movement actions

 Practise hopping like Rabbit Foo Foo to the sound of a tambour, drum or woodblock. Practise fluttering and dancing to a quiet tinkling sound. Put the two instruments where they can't be seen (e.g. on the floor behind an up-ended table). Ask the children to move like rabbits or fairies depending on the sound they hear. There should be no talking. When the sound stops, the children stop.

▶ Vary the speed and volume of playing to get more subtle variations of movement. For example, quiet, slow taps on the tambour should produce small, slow hops. A loud and rapid trill on the triangle should produce vigorous flying.

▶ For a more advanced version of the game you will need two people to make the sounds, one for each instrument. Ask the rest of the children to decide whether to be rabbits or fairies – no changing minds! Tell the children to hop or fly only when they hear their sound. Start off by playing the sounds one at a time. When the children are responding well, play them together. Finally, try a combination of single sounds and two sounds together.

Let's make magic

game to practise loud and soft sounds

 Sit half the children in a large fairy ring. Give each 'fairy' a tinkling or chiming instrument. Ask them to make, in turn, quiet magic, loud magic, loud magic getting quieter and quiet magic getting louder. The rest of the 'fairies' go into the middle of the ring and dance to the magic: gently when it's quiet, more vigorously when it's loud, and so on. Swap over.

Five little owls

game poem with sound effects

Five little owls in an old elm tree,
Fluffy and puffy as owls could be,
Blinking and winking with big round eyes
At the big round moon that hung in the skies.
As I passed beneath I could hear one say,
'There'll be mouse for supper, there will today!'
Then all of them hooted, 'Tu-whit, Tu-whoo!
Yes, mouse for supper, Hoo-hoo, Hoo-hoo!'

Barbara Ireson

▶ Ask five children to be owls. Sit them in a row on tables, chairs or a bench. Ask them to hoot at the appropriate time.

▶ Make the poem into a game by asking one owl to fly away at the end of each reading. Choose five children to be mice on the woodland floor. They can be caught (squeaking) one at a time, until there are no owls and no mice left.

Little Red Riding Hood

traditional story with woodland sound effects

Tell the story of Little Red Riding Hood. Talk about some of the sounds she might have heard in the wood on the way to Grandma's house: woodpecker, rustling leaves, cuckoo, axe, whistling blackbird. Find ways to make the sounds using voices, instruments or anything else that you may have to hand (e.g. crumpled tissue paper for leaves).

▶ Paint a large picture to show Red Riding Hood's route through the trees. Include a woodpecker, cuckoo and other birds. Everyone can make a tree to stick on the picture. Cut Red Riding Hood out of card and mount her on a stick. Move her along the path and make her stop and listen to the sounds of the wood. You could also cut out and mount the other key figures from the story (wolf, grandmother, woodcutter) and include them in the action.

Trees

song about trees in all four seasons

In the Autumn leaves are falling,
Brown, brown, leaves are falling.
In the Autumn leaves are falling,
Falling from the trees.

In the Winter leaves are sleeping,
Brown, brown, leaves are sleeping.
In the Winter leaves are sleeping,
Sleeping in the trees.

In the Spring the leaves are budding,
Green, green, leaves are budding.
In the Spring the leaves are budding,
Budding on the trees.

In the Summer leaves are rustling,
Green, green, leaves are rustling.
In the Summer leaves are rustling,
Rustling on the trees.

In the Au-tumn leaves are fal-ling, Brown, brown, leaves are fal-ling. In the Au-tumn leaves are fal-ling, Fal-ling from the trees.

Music Box tape

listening and joining in

Down in the forest

Listen to the song and enjoy the image of an elephant washing his clothes in the forest. Sway slowly from side to side in time to the beat. Practise the nonsense words of the chorus, slowly. Rub hands together on the 'rub-a-dubs'. When you know the song quite well, replace the elephant with other animals: crocodile, wombat, tiger.

▶ Make up new verses to include other woodland animals (e.g. owl, squirrel, woodlouse, woodpecker, worm). Another time sing about animals from a different habitat (e.g. tigers, parrots, crocodiles).

More ideas

▶ Tell the story of Hansel and Gretel.

▶ Read the story *Goodnight Owl* by Pat Hutchins (Picture Puffin, 1975).

▶ Read the counting poem 'One little brown bird' from *Knock at the door*.

▶ Sing and mime to 'In a cottage in a wood' from *Okki-tokki-unga*.

Cross-curricular links

Language

▶ What happens to Rabbit Foo Foo after the Good Fairy has changed him into something else? Does he run away and hide? Does he become even more naughty and start attacking larger animals? Does he promise to be good and get another chance? Does he redeem himself by performing some heroic deed? Ask the children to continue the story.

▶ Talk about animal sounds. For example, a mouse squeaks, an owl hoots, a badger snuffles and a fox barks.

Maths

▶ Sort a collection of autumnal seeds and nuts, such as conkers, acorns, sycamore seeds and beech casts.

▶ Put three oranges on one plate and one apple on another. How many pieces of fruit altogether (touch and count)? Which plate has the most fruit? Check by counting and matching. Try this with other fruits and change the number of items on the plates.

Science

▶ Collect lots of fallen leaves. Put them in a big box or basket and ask the children to feel them and to move them around. Look at the colours, patterns and shapes. Ask each child to choose five (or more) leaves and to arrange them on a piece of paper. Encourage them to try all sorts of arrangements. Let them change their leaves. Give them a choice of paper shape (e.g. square, long and thin, circular, triangular) and paper colour. Take individual photographs of the final leaf arrangements.

▶ When the children have finished with the leaves, dig a hole in the ground and put the leaves in it. Cover with soil and mark the spot. Ask the children what they think will happen to the leaves. Dig them up in a month's time to see if they were right. Look again a month later. Do the same with apple peel (see 'Cookery'), apple cores, orange peel and banana skins. If you can't bury the leaves or fruit in the ground, put them in a see-through plastic bag, add water and seal. Watch what happens to the contents.

▶ Ask the children to look out for and bring in different seeds, such as conkers, acorns and sycamore seeds. Put them on paper plates, one for each seed type, and look carefully – through a magnifying glass, if possible. Talk about their shape, colour, weight and size. Throw the sycamore seeds into the air and watch them spin to the ground.

Art and craft

▶ Use large paper plates to make owls. Paint the plates brown and cut out and stick on big round yellow eyes, triangular beaks and pointed ears. Stick feathers on wings made out of card and then attach them to the sides of the plates.

▶ Make a tree which is taller than the children. Use a strong cardboard tube for the trunk and wedge it upright between heavy objects or wedge it over a weighted rounders post. Drape with brown or green material or crepe paper. Push painted cardboard branches or real twigs into slits or holes up the trunk. Stick on lots of brown, red, green and orange leaves, and scatter some on the floor. Make a squirrel or two to sit in the branches. Put mice at the base of the tree, and let a fox peep round the trunk.

Cookery

▶ Make apple crumble. If you have any brambles near you, pick some blackberries and add them to the apples. ●

Magic machines

craft activity with mechanical sound effects

▶ Make a collection of machines (e.g. hairdrier, tape recorder, electric kettle, sewing machine, torch and typewriter). Talk about the machines in your collection. Draw or paint them. What makes them work? What do they do? Who uses them? How do you make them start? Do you plug them in, press a switch, turn a knob, wind them up or press a foot pedal?

▶ Help the children to make their own magic machines. First of all decide what the magic machines will do: fly you to the moon, make breakfast, tidy your toys, do sums, cook biscuits, turn buttons into pennies, make things change colour.

▶ Start with a large box. Add wires, plugs, switches and knobs. Use split pins to make knobs or dials that turn. Push lolly sticks into slots to make levers that move up and down. Coloured plastic lids make good lights. Use pipe cleaners for wires. Label switches 'on' and 'off'. Push a cardboard tube through the machine and label one end 'in' and the other 'out'. Decorate the machine with foil, glitter and tinsel to make it look magic.

▶ Talk about and play with the machines. Let each child experiment with instruments and other sound-making equipment to produce two or three mechanical sounds. The junk box can be a good source of sounds: pop the bubbles in clear plastic packaging; drag a ruler over corrugated card; make high and low beeping sounds through tubes; clip plastic pots together; rattle buttons in plastic tubs; tap cardboard and plastic boxes. Can the children make clicks, winding-up sounds, engine sounds, beeps, rattles, whirring sounds and bangs and pops?

▶ Listen to the different sounds and talk about them. Are they loud or soft or in between? Are they high or low or can't you tell? Are they smooth or wobbly? Are they fast or slow? Do they last a long time or are they short? Are they regular or do they only happen now and then?

▶ Ask the children to draw their magic machines, showing the sounds coming from them.

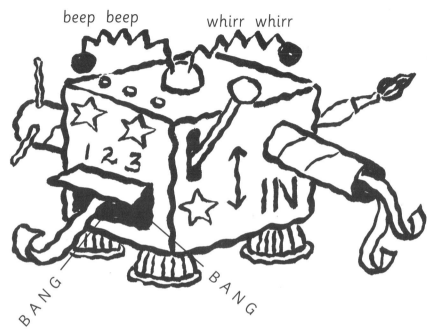

beep beep   whirr whirr

BANG   BANG

▶ Invite the children to make up a story about their machines and incorporate the mechanical sounds. For example:

'This is my magic machine. When you switch it on like this (mouth click) it starts making magic (tambourine rattle). It's making a milk shake for me. Here it comes into a beaker (watery sound made by scrunching tissue paper). Yum yum, that was delicious. Now I'll switch it off (mouth click).'

Or:

'This is my magic machine. It turns pebbles into conkers. First I'll wind it up (scraping sound made with a guiro). Turn on the beeper (beep-beep mouth sound) and put a pebble in the 'in' hole. Now wait for the magic (tinkling sound made by rubbing a beater over a glockenspiel) . . . and out comes the conker (popping sound made with finger in cheek).'

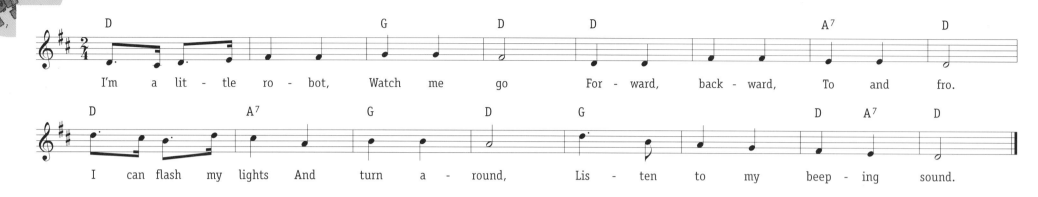

I'm a lit - tle ro - bot, Watch me go For - ward, back - ward, To and fro.

I can flash my lights And turn a - round, Lis - ten to my beep - ing sound.

I'm a little robot

action song with sound effects

I'm a little robot
Watch me go
Forward, backward,
To and fro.
I can flash my light
And turn round,
Listen to my beeping* sound . . . beep beep beep beep.

▶ Sing the song to the tune of 'I'm a little teapot'. Move around the room like a robot: forwards, backwards and round about. At the end of each verse the children make mechanical sounds with voices or sound-makers. Continue to move around while the sounds are made. Move smoothly during the purring, make strong jerky movements to the banging, turn pretend handles or twirl around to the whirring, and so on.

Little robot

poem with movement and sound effects

I'm a little robot,
Wires make me talk.
I'm a little robot,
Wires make me walk.
I'm a little robot,
Wires bend my knees.
I'm a little robot,
Wires make me sneeze.
AAAACHOOOOOOOO!
I'm a little robot,
Wires make me work.
So if you ever cross them,
I'll probably go BERSERK!
ZOING ZOING BOINK!
ZOING ZOING BOINK!
ZING!

Robert Heidbreder

* whirring, clanking, banging, purring, tooting

▶ Join in the last three lines of the poem. Make voices match the sounds.

▶ Find instruments for the three sounds: ZOING, BOINK and ZING. Choose a player for each and play the pattern:

ZOING ZOING BOINK!
ZOING ZOING BOINK!
ZING!

I am a robot

rhythmic chanting game using symbols

 Practise chanting 'I am a robot' in a flat, dalek-like voice. Clap as you chant (one clap per symbol). Count the claps.

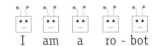

I   am   a   ro - bot

▶ Make up some more robot chants and accompany with claps, shakes or taps. For example:

I   can bend   my   legs

I   have   a   flash-ing   light

My name   is   Ro -bert*   Ro - bot

I   am made   of   me - tal

I   have   lots   of   swit-ches

Music Box tape

listening and joining in

I'm walking like a robot

Listen to the song a few times and then add actions in a standing position. Try to keep in time with the slow beat of the music. Move feet up and down on the spot as you walk 'like a robot'. Move one arm up and down stiffly as you pretend to brush your teeth. Turn your head quickly from side to side in the third verse. Finally, press pretend buttons on your chest.

More ideas

▶ There is a range of brightly illustrated poems in *Machine poems,* collected by Jill Bennett (Oxford University Press, 1993).

▶ *Music through topics* has a section called 'At home' which includes activities based on sounds in the kitchen.

▶ *This little puffin . . .* includes several rhymes and songs about clocks, tractors and kitchen and garden equipment.

▶ Read *Doing the washing* by Sarah Garland (Puffin, 1995).

* substitute for name of child in group

Cross-curricular links

Language

▶ Make a collection of objects which make interesting sounds. Find a word to describe each sound. For example:

balloon	*POP!*
biscuit wrapping	*crackle*
large pan and wooden spoon	*BANG!*
dry twig	*snap*
bowl of dry cornflakes	*crunch*
two yoghurt pots	*clip clop*
party blower	*WHEE!*
coins	*jingle*

▶ Make a label for each sound. Use capital letters to denote LOUD sounds. Let the writing and shape of the labels reflect the sound.

▶ Ask the children, one at a time, to pretend to use a household machine such as a hair-drier, vacuum cleaner, torch or typewriter. Can anyone guess what is going on?

Maths

▶ Make pictograms or block graphs to show the machines found in the children's kitchens/living rooms/bedrooms.

▶ Make a collection of weighing machines (e.g. balances, kitchen and bathroom scales). Talk about them. What are they for? Why do we need to find out how much things weigh? Put a variety of objects on the kitchen equipment and watch what happens. Let the children take it in turns to stand on the bathroom scales and watch the pointer move.

▶ Play the game 'Just a minute'. You will need a stopwatch or kitchen timer. Find out how many times the children can draw a cross, write their name, bounce a ball or run and pick up a bean bag in one minute. Make up your own 'minute' games. Older children can keep records and try to improve their personal performances. Can the children sit quietly for one minute?

Science

▶ Look at a variety of clocks and timers. Talk about their appearance and function. Why is a wristwatch small? Why has a kitchen timer got a loud alarm? Group them to show those that are powered by clockwork, electicity, battery, microchip or other (e.g. sand timer). Which ones make a sound? Listen to the alarms. Copy the sounds using voices.

▶ Look at and talk about the machines at your playgroup or school. Draw them. Warn children about the dangers of electricty. Keep an eye open for machines in shops, towns, parks and on farms.

Art and craft

▶ Work together to make a large robot. Start with a box big enough to accommodate a child. Paint it and make a hole or a door at the back for easy access. Use cardboard tubes for arms and rubber gloves for hands. Stick antennae (wire clothes hangers with foam balls stuck on the ends) on the head. Can you fix the head so that it revolves? Older children can use electrical equipment to make a beeper. Stick a variety of objects on the body for switches and dials.

▶ How can you make the robot move around the room (e.g. get inside and push, drag it along on a piece of card or material, pull it with string)? Can the child inside the robot follow simple instructions: start, stop, go forward, go backward, turn right, turn left, pause? ●

WINTER

Peace at last

story by Jill Murphy

The hour was late. Mr Bear was tired, Mrs Bear was tired and Baby Bear was tired, so they all went to bed.

Mrs Bear fell asleep. Mr Bear didn't. Mrs Bear began to snore.

'Snore,' went Mrs Bear, 'SNORE, SNORE, SNORE.'

'Oh NO!' said Mr Bear, 'I can't stand THIS.'

So he got up and went to sleep in Baby Bear's room.

Baby Bear was not asleep either. He was lying in bed pretending to be an aeroplane.

'NYAAOW!' went Baby Bear, 'NYAAOW! NYAAOW!'

'Oh NO!' said Mr Bear, 'I can't stand THIS.'

So he got up and went to sleep in the living-room.

TICK-TOCK . . . went the living-room clock . . . . TICK-TOCK, TICK-TOCK. CUCKOO! CUCKOO!

'Oh NO!' said Mr Bear, 'I can't stand THIS.'

So he went off to sleep in the kitchen.

DRIP, DRIP . . . went the leaky kitchen tap.

HMMMMMMMMMMM . . . went the refrigerator.

'Oh NO,' said Mr Bear, 'I can't stand THIS.'

So he got up and went to sleep in the garden.

Well, you would not believe what noises there are in the garden at night.

'TOO-WHIT-TOO-WHOO!' went the owl.

'SNUFFLE, SNUFFLE,' went the hedgehog.

'MIAAAOW!' sang the cats on the wall.

'Oh, NO!' said Mr Bear, 'I can't stand THIS.'

So he went off to sleep in the car.

It was cold in the car and uncomfortable, but Mr Bear was so tired that he didn't notice. He was just falling asleep when all the birds started to sing and the sun peeped in at the window.

'TWEET TWEET!' went the birds.

SHINE, SHINE . . . went the sun.

'Oh NO!' said Mr Bear, 'I can't stand THIS.'

So he got up and went back into the house.

In the house, Baby Bear was fast asleep, and Mrs Bear had turned over and wasn't snoring any more. Mr Bear got into bed and closed his eyes.

'Peace at last,' he said to himself.

BRRRRRRRRRRRRRRRR! went the alarm-clock, BRRRRRR!

Mrs Bear sat up and rubbed her eyes.

'Good morning, dear,' she said. 'Did you sleep well?'

'Not VERY well, dear,' yawned Mr Bear.

'Never mind,' said Mrs Bear. 'I'll bring you a nice cup of tea.'

And she did.

▶ Before reading the story *Peace at last* by Jill Murphy talk about going to bed. Make a collection of pyjamas, nighties, hot-water bottles, favourite toys, night-lights and storybooks. Who puts the children to bed? Does anyone say a bedtime prayer or sing a bedtime song? What sort of beds do the children sleep in? Who shares a bedroom? Does anyone find it hard to get to sleep, and, if so, why?

Sound pictures

first attempts at scoring using pictures and symbols

 Tell the children that you are going to *draw* some of the sounds in the story. You will need a large piece of paper and a felt-tip.

▶ Mrs Bear snores. Do the children know anyone who snores? Ask for demonstrations. All snore together. Snore on the in-breath, then puff noisily on the out-breath. Talk about the snores. Are they smooth or wobbly? Make a snoring sound with a guiro. Draw the sound.

▶ Baby Bear pretends to be an aeroplane. Invite children to make aeroplane sounds. Encourage sounds which rise and dip. Draw the sound.

▶ The living room clock ticks. Ask everyone to make the sound of a ticking clock. Accompany with a finger movement from side to side. Try to keep together. Add a woodblock accompaniment. Is it a long or short sound? Does it go all over the place like the aeroplane noise or does it stay the same? Practise the 'cuckoo'. Draw the sounds. Show the drop in pitch.

tick - tock tick - tock tick - tock tick - tock

 cuc koo   cuc koo

▶ The tap drips. Who can make a dripping sound? (Smack the tongue against the top of the mouth just behind the teeth.) Is it loud or quiet? Pretend to be lots of dripping taps – no need to stay together. Draw the sound.

▶ The refrigerator hums. Ask everyone to hum quietly. Is it a long or short sound? Draw it.

▶ Other sounds in the story include a hooting owl, a snuffling hedgehog, a miaowing cat and the dawn chorus. Just as Mr Bear falls asleep, the alarm goes off. Imitate all these sounds.

▶ The next time you tell the story choose individual children to make all the sounds except the dawn chorus and the alarm clock, which can be made by everyone.

▶ If you have a copy of the book *Peace at last* by Jill Murphy (Macmillan, 1995), display it with a collection of sound-makers. Encourage the children to make the relevant sound effects as they look through the book.

Sound lotto

sound discrimination game

Make a set of sound lotto boards using eight of the sounds in the story: snore, aeroplane, tap, ticking clock, fridge, cat, alarm, owl. Make a tape of the eight sounds (vocal imitations). Ask the children to put counters on the pictures as they recognise the sounds.

snore	roar	drip	tick
hum	miaow	brrrr	hoot

Shake and play

game to practise quiet playing and careful handling of instruments

Sit in a circle. Give a tambourine to one of the children. Shake a big dice. If the number is five, the tambourine is passed round five children. The aim is to be as quiet as possible. The fifth child taps the tambourine very quietly five times. Shake the dice again and continue as before. Try the game with jingle bells or maracas. Older children can have two or more instruments on the go at the same time. They should play together.

Quiet sounds

game to practise quiet instrumental playing

Sit in a circle and give everyone an instrument to play. Include home-made ones. If you haven't got enough instruments, sit half the children on chairs in a circle and the rest on the floor inside the circle. Those on chairs take it in turns with those on the floor to play the instruments. The first child plays his or her instrument very quietly for as long as he or she wants to. As soon as the sound stops, the next child plays, and so on. Instruments can be tapped, shaken, scraped or blown. Children waiting to play should keep their instruments very still. Remember, *still* means *quiet*!

Bedtime whispers

game to practise quiet, slow speaking

Decide on a bedtime message to be passed round the circle, such as 'Go to sleep', 'Close your eyes' or 'Rock-a-bye baby'. Talk about the sort of voice you would use: quiet, soothing, slow. If you have a lot of children, change the message once it has been repeated about ten times.

Wake up!

game to practise loud, quick speaking

What sort of voice would you use if you were trying to wake someone up? Play as for 'Bedtime whispers' but this time pass round 'Wake up' or 'Time for school' or 'Wakey wakey!' Use loud voices, but don't shout!

Loud and soft

game to practise patterns of loud and quiet speaking and playing

 Sit in a circle. Choose two contrasing messages to pass round – one loud, the other quiet – such as 'Go to sleep' and 'Wake up!' The first child begins with a quiet 'Go to sleep', followed by a loud 'Wake up!' from the second child. Carry on round the circle.

▶ Now try with instruments. You may need to sit in two circles (see 'Quiet sounds'). The first instrument is played quietly. As soon as the sound ends, the next child plays his or her instrument loudly, and so on.

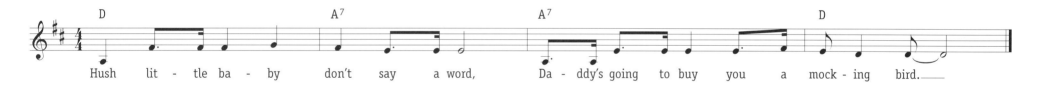

Hush lit - tle ba - by don't say a word, Da - ddy's going to buy you a mock - ing bird.

Hush little baby

lullaby to sing

 Hush little baby don't say a word,
Daddy's (Mummy's) going to buy you a mocking bird.

If that mocking bird won't sing,
Daddy's going to buy you a diamond ring.

If that diamond ring is brass,
Daddy's going to buy you a looking-glass.

If that looking-glass gets broke,
Daddy's going to buy you a billy-goat.

If that billy-goat won't pull,
Daddy's going to buy you a cart and bull.

If that cart and bull turn over,
Daddy's going to buy you a dog called Rover.

If that dog called Rover won't bark,
Daddy's going to buy you a horse and cart.

If that horse and cart fall down,
You'll still be the sweetest little baby in town.

▶ Sing other lullabies, such as 'Rock-a-bye baby'. Encourage the children to rock a toy as they sing and to move their bodies in time with the music.

Music Box tape

listening and joining in

Get in the bath

Listen to the song a few times and talk about bathtime. Join in with 'splish splash' and 'glug glug'. In the first verse the children can pretend to wash themselves. In the second verse they can dry themselves. Older children can touch the various parts of the body as they are mentioned. At the end of the song ask the children to lie on the floor and to pretend to go to sleep.

Hushabye

Ask the children to close their eyes and to sit still as they listen to this soothing lullabye. Listen out for the humming – it copies the tune. Hum the tune of other well-known lullabies.

More ideas

▶ Read *The princess and the pea* by Hans Christian Andersen (Longman, 1986).

▶ Read *Can't you sleep little bear?* by Martin Waddell (Walker, 1990).

▶ Read *Dinosaur dreams* by Alan Ahlberg and Andre Amstutz (Mammoth, 1992).

Cross-curricular links

Language

▶ Make the play corner into a bedroom with a bed, hot-water bottle, toys, pyjamas, nighties, slippers and books. Three children can act out the story *Peace at last* by Jill Murphy. Embellish the story. Baby Bear, for example, can have a bath and bedtime story. Add sound effects.

▶ Talk about dreams – nice and not-so-nice ones. Read *Mog the forgetful cat* by Judith Kerr (HarperCollins, 1993) and talk about the people in the story.

Maths

▶ Do some bedtime research and record the results using pictograms or sets.

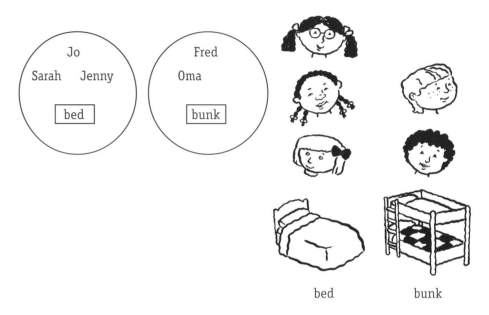

Other themes: shares a bedroom — has his/her own bedroom
wears pyjamas — wears a nightie
likes going to bed — doesn't like going to bed

▶ Sing and act out the traditional song 'There were ten in the bed' (younger children can start with five). Pause after the line 'There were . . . in the bed' and count the children lying on the floor. Practise counting backwards.

▶ Talk about bedtimes. Older children can look at and make o'clock bedtimes on large clocks. How many hours are you asleep?

Science

▶ Talk about day and night, the sun and the moon. Draw pictures of things you do in the day and things you do at night. Talk about people who work during the night.

▶ Talk about animals that come out at night, such as owls, hedgehogs, bats and snails. Look at picture books to find out more information about these animals. What do they look like? What do they eat? Where do they live? How do they move? Why are they nocturnal?

Art and craft

▶ Uses boxes to make beds for favourite toys. Match the size of the toy to the size of the box. Stick on bed legs and paint or make bars on cots. Cut up material for bedclothes. Use old tights to stuff pillows. Play games with the toys and beds using vocabulary of size: 'Your bed is too short for my teddy', 'This bed is too small for your doll.' Put three or four beds in order of length, starting with the shortest. Which beds are the same size?

Drama

▶ Talk about getting ready for bed. What do you do first of all? Mime taking off shoes and socks (e.g. undo laces, unfasten velcro or buckles). Mime taking off other clothes (e.g. undo buttons and zips). Put on night clothes. Wash and dry hands and face. Comb hair. Clean teeth. Snuggle down and go to sleep.

▶ Invite the children, one at a time, to mime any one of the above activities. The other children guess the action.

Cookery

▶ Make bedtime drinks using hot milk. What happens to the powder when mixed with the milk?

▶ Start the day with breakfast, inviting parents/helpers/teachers along. What are cereals made of? What happens to the cereal when milk is added? Make toast. Talk about the changes to the bread: colour, texture, temperature, taste. Spread with jam, marmalade or honey. Talk about the source of the sweet spreads, i.e. fruit and bee hives. Clean teeth. ●

Whatever next?

story by Jill Murphy

'Can I go to the moon?' asked Baby Bear.

'No you can't,' said Mrs Bear. 'It's bathtime. Anyway, you'd have to find a rocket first.'

Baby Bear found a rocket in the cupboard under the stairs. He found a space-helmet on the draining board in the kitchen, and a pair of space-boots on the mat by the front door. He packed his teddy and some food for the journey and took off up the chimney . . . WHOOSH! Out into the night.

An owl flew past.

'That's a smart rocket,' he said. 'Where are you off to?'

'The moon,' said Baby Bear. 'Would you like to come too?'

'Yes please,' said the owl.

An aeroplane roared out of the clouds. Baby Bear waved and some of the passengers waved back.

On and on they flew, up and up, above the clouds, past millions of stars till at last they landed on the moon.

'There's nobody here,' said Baby Bear.

'There's no trees,' said the owl.

'It's a bit boring,' said Baby Bear. 'Shall we have a picnic?'

'What a good idea,' said the owl.

'We'd better go,' said Baby Bear. 'My bath must be ready by now.'

Off they went, down and down. The owl got out and flew away.

'Goodbye,' he said. 'It was so nice to meet you.'

It rained and the rain dripped through Baby Bear's helmet.

Home went Baby Bear. Back down the chimney and on to the living room carpet with a BUMP!

Mrs Bear came into the room.

'Look at the state of you!' she gasped as she led him away to the bathroom. 'Why, you look as if you've been up the chimney.'

'As a matter of fact,' said Baby Bear, 'I have been up the chimney. I found a rocket and went to visit the moon.'

Mrs Bear laughed.

'You and your stories,' she said. 'Whatever next?'

▶ Read *Whatever next?* by Jill Murphy and add sound effects.

Sound effects

Baby Bear assembles his equipment for going to the moon. Space helmet on head, space boots on feet, teddy and food stashed away in his rocket, he prepares for take-off.

▶ Ask the children how they can make a roaring sound to describe the rocket blasting into space. Experiment with mouth sounds and with instrumental sounds. Find ways to produce a LOUD sound. Try starting quietly, get louder, sustain the loud sound, then fade as the rocket moves away from Earth. Start with a countdown: 10 9 8 7 6 5 4 3 2 1 0. Let everyone join in. Keep together.

▶ Experiment with voices, instruments and other sound-makers to make a sound picture of outer space. First set the scene. What will Baby Bear see as he shoots through the sky? Try to create a feeling of coldness, darkness, twinkling stars and meteors. Involve all the children. Use the space music to accompany Baby Bear's return to Earth later on in the story.

▶ Make flapping and hooting sounds for the owl and a roaring sound for the plane. Think about volume (loud or quiet) and duration (length of sound).

▶ Try lots of ways to make the sound of rain: quiet smacking of tongue against top of mouth; finger clicks; fingernails tapped on floor, furniture, card or paper; shakers; woodblocks. Listen to the sounds and talk about them. Is it a heavy shower of rain or just a few drops? Discuss how many people should be involved in making the rain sounds.

▶ Experiment with voices to make the sound of the descent down the chimney. End with a BUMP!

▶ Make the sound of water running into the bath.

▶ Finish with everyone joining Mrs Bear as she says, 'Whatever next?'

▶ Make picture cards for the various sound effects and display them on a table with a selection of sound-makers. If you have a copy of the book *Whatever next!* by Jill Murphy (Macmillan, 1995), put that out instead of the cards. Encourage the children to use either the cards or the book illustrations to prompt sound effects. Perhaps one child could tell the story from memory while two others add the sound effects.

Lift off

game practising a rising sequence of notes (getting higher)

 Young children often find it difficult to distinguish between sounds getting higher and sounds getting lower. Games such as 'Lift off' and 'Splash down' will help them to differentiate between rising and falling pitch.

▶ Tip and support a pitched percussion instrument (xylophone/glockenspiel) on one end, long bars nearest the floor. Tap each bar in turn, slowly, starting with the lowest note (longest bar). The notes get higher. Do this several times and ask them to listen carefully to the rising effect. Then ask the children to mime a rocket taking off using their hands. Put both hands together, fingers pointing to the ceiling. Start low and move the playing upwards, until the children's hands are above their heads.

▶ Enlarge the pictorial sound sequence and display in the music corner with a pitched percussion instrument. Encourage the children, solo or in pairs, to translate the pictures into sounds. You may want to include a sound-maker for the BOOM!

Splash down

game practising a falling seuence of notes (getting lower)

 As for 'Lift off', but this time tap the bars in the opposite direction, starting at the top with the highest or shortest bar and moving down to the lowest note. Ask the children to imagine a space capsule falling from the sky and landing in the pond. Use hands to mime the landing. Start high and land with a SPLASH! on thighs.

▶ Enlarge the pictorial sound sequence below and display in the music corner with a pitched percussion instrument. Encourage the children, solo or in pairs, to translate the pictures into sounds. Include a sound-maker for the SPLASH!

	SPLASH 	HOORAY! 

Five little astronauts

action poem

 Five little astronauts
Rocketing through space.
One missed her/his teddy bear
And shuttled back to base.

THAT LEFT FOUR

Four little astronauts
Rocketing through space.
One had a tummy ache
And shuttled back to base.

THAT LEFT THREE

Three little astronauts
Rocketing through space.
One wanted fish and chips
And shuttled back to base.

THAT LEFT TWO

Two little astronauts
Rocketing through space.
One couldn't get to sleep
And shuttled back to base.

THAT LEFT ONE

One little astronaut
Rocketing through space.
She/he got lonely
And shuttled back to base.

▶ Chant the poem several times and act it out with five children and a pretend spaceship. After the last line of each verse, play from high to low on a pitched percussion instrument or keyboard and make a splashing sound as the shuttle falls into the sea.

Space chants

clapping and chanting rhythms

Try these space chants. Aim to speak together. Accompany the rhythm of the words with either body or instrumental sounds. The symbols above the words indicate the rhythm, i.e. one clap/tap/shake/scrape per symbol. Think about volume. Keep the speed slow.

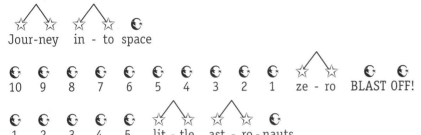

Jour-ney in - to space

10 9 8 7 6 5 4 3 2 1 ze - ro BLAST OFF!

1 2 3 4 5 lit - tle ast - ro - nauts

Spaceship to the moon

action song

Shuma has a spaceship that will take us to the moon,
Shuma has a spaceship that will take us to the moon,
Shuma has a spaceship that will take us to the moon,
So we climb in, press the switch, and ZOOOOM!

We can walk around in spaceboots,
We can walk around in spaceboots,
We can walk around in spaceboots,
We're walking on the moon.

David has a spaceship that will take us to the moon . . .
We can ride off in our buggy,
We can ride off in our buggy,
We can ride off in our buggy,
We're riding on the moon.

Sally has a spaceship that will take us to the moon . . .
We can jump across the craters,
We can jump across the craters,
We can jump across the craters,
We're jumping on the moon.

▶ Sing the song to the tune of 'John Brown's body'.

▶ In the first stanza stride slowly around in pretend moonboots. In the second stanza sit in pairs, one behind the other, and bounce up and down in a pretend buggy. Finally, jump across moon craters.

Music Box tape

listening and joining in

I'm a green spaceman
Get to know the song and talk about the space words. Listen out for the mysterious introductory music and accompaniment.

More ideas

▶ Sing the old favourite 'Twinkle twinkle little star' to a background accompaniment of silvery sounds.

▶ Sing the nursery rhyme 'Hey diddle diddle'. Use a swanee whistle to describe the jump over the moon.

▶ Read the story *But Martin* by June Counsel (Corgi, 1986) and then talk about it.

▶ Read *Meg on the moon* by Helen Nicoll and Jan Pienkowski (Picture Puffin, 1976).

Cross-curricular links

Language

▶ The green spacemen on the *Music Box* tape spoke gobbledegook. Ask the children to make up some gobbledegook words and sounds.

Maths

▶ Make rockets out of cardboard tubes. Try to get a variety of heights and widths. Which is the tallest, fattest, thinnest and shortest? Paint and decorate the tubes and attach egg-box cones on the top. Cover with foil and add tissue paper flames.

▶ Prepare to launch the rockets. Make a collection of things that produce loud sounds, such as saucepan lids, cymbals, tambourines and tambours. Count backwards from ten. On zero make the sound of a rocket taking off. Children without sound-makers can make explosion noises using their voices. Try counting backwards from six or from numbers greater than ten.

▶ Make pretend fireworks. Collect small boxes and tubes and talk about their shape. Which ones are round? Can you see a square on your box? Count the corners. Decorate the fireworks with foil. Add crepe paper streamers and tissue flames.

Science

▶ Find different ways of launching the rockets. Lift or throw them up in the air. Catapult them up using a see-saw device. Experiment with rubber bands.

▶ Talk about the sky and outer space. Why is the sky black at night? What do you know about the sun?

▶ Is the sun always in the same place? Is the moon always the same shape?

Art and craft

▶ Listen to the song 'I'm a green spaceman' on the tape. Talk about the colours: green astronaut, red planet, blue trees and birds. The astronaut has pointy ears and 29 toes. Make pictures (or one large picture) of the astronaut using paint, crayons, string, wool, lolly sticks and silver foil.

▶ Build a spaceship. Use huge cardboard boxes (washing-machine size) or rolls of corrugated card for the rocket. Make a door and windows. Use colanders or cut up old plastic footballs for space helmets. Wellies make good moonboots. Pretend space food can be made from straws and small plastic bags. Make a switchboard using lids and bottle tops. Paint a space backdrop. Splatter multi-coloured stars all over the paper. Cut out a moon and make egg-box craters. A battery operated walkie-talkie can be the link with planet Earth. Talk in gobbledegook. ●

JINGLE BELLS

Bell collection
listening to a range of chiming sounds

Make a collection of bells (e.g. cowbells, hand bells, angel chimes, mobiles, toys, socks with bells, old-fashioned school bells). Shake them, describe their sound and talk about the material from which they are made. Are they magnetic? What are they used for?

Bell circle
instrumental playing skills

 Sit in a large circle and give each child a bell to play. Use the bells in your collection (see above) and supplement with hand jingles and sleigh bells. Take it in turns to shake them. Each child plays for as long as he or she wants to, with the next person following on as soon as the sound stops.

▶ Take it in turns to play loudly. Take it in turns to play quietly. Alternate loud and quiet.

▶ Each child plays for a long time. Each child plays for a short time. Alternate long and short.

Guess the bell
sound discrimination game

 Choose two contrasting bells from the collection and put them behind a screen (e.g. an up-ended table). One child goes behind the screen and shakes one of the bells. The other children have to say which one has been played. The first child to get it right has the next turn at shaking one of the bells. Make the game more difficult by using three or four different bells.

Jingle bells
song with jingle bell accompaniment

 Jingle bells, jingle bells,
Jingle all the way.
Oh what fun it is to ride
On a one-horse open sleigh.
OH!
Jingle bells, jingle bells,
Jingle all the way.
Oh what fun it is ro ride
On a one-horse open sleigh.

▶ Sing the song 'Jingle bells', slowly at first. Accompany with jingle sticks – one per child, if possible. Two each would be even better – one in each hand. Jingle sticks are cheap to buy and easy to make (see 'Art and craft'). The song has a strong beat and many of the children will be able to play in time with the singing. Give a strong lead. Encourage the children to bob gently up and down on their bottoms in time with the shaking.

Santa's sleigh

game with jingle bells to practise getting faster and slower, quieter and louder

Show the children a picture of a sleigh pulled by reindeer. Talk about different ways of travelling across snow: skis, sledges, sleighs, toboggans. What makes the various things move: sticks, horses, reindeer, dogs? Talk about Father Christmas' sleigh.

▶ Make a pretend sleigh using an upturned table. Sit one child (Father Christmas) on a chair on the sledge. The rest of the children, in pairs, are the reindeer. Give each reindeer one or two jingle sticks.

▶ Father Christmas is setting off on his rounds on Christmas Eve. Shake the jingle sticks slowly at first, get faster and faster, then settle to a quiet, continuous jingling as the sleigh takes off and flies through the air. Fade out as it disappears into the distance. Now make the sound of the sleigh returning to Greenland and landing. Start quietly and get louder as the sleigh approaches the landing point. Slow down and stop. Finish with a few moments of silence.

The magic sleigh bell

story with sleigh bell sound effects

It was Christmas Eve and, wonder of wonders, it was snowing. Millions and millions of feathery flakes drifted down from the starry sky. They landed silently on roof-tops, tree-tops and on the tops of cars, until the ground was covered with a crunchy white carpet of ice. The children watched from their windows, round-eyed and excited.

Far away in Greenland, Father Christmas was struggling to get everything ready for his round-the-world trip. His huge sack of toys was wedged in the back of the sleigh and the reindeer were harnessed and ready to go. Father Christmas wrapped his blanket round his knees and pulled on the reins. Slowly at first, then faster and faster, the reindeer ran across the snow (1). The merry sound of the sleigh bells rang out in the frosty night air. The reindeer pulled away up into the sky, and Father Christmas settled down for the long ride ahead of him (2).

* substitute for name of your own village, town or city

In Bolton* the children were busy wrapping up presents, hanging up stockings, writing letters to Father Christmas and running to the window every few moments to look at the snow. One by one they went to bed, and one by one they fell asleep.

One little girl – her name was Debbie – lay awake for a long time. She very much wanted to stay awake and see Father Christmas. She wanted to know what he looked like, and she had a lot of questions to ask him. She opened her curtains and looked out at the snowflakes which danced past her window. She crawled to the end of her bed to feel her empty stocking. Dad came in and gave her a kiss. At last, too tired to stay awake any longer, she fell asleep.

Much later Debbie woke up with a start. Something had disturbed her sleep – a jingly sort of sound. She opened her eyes wide and listened. She felt her way to the window and peered outside. It had stopped snowing and the moon was shining as bright as day. Debbie shivered then yawned. She climbed back into bed and pulled her duvet up over her shoulders. A few moments later she was fast asleep.

Christmas Day dawned white and clear. Debbie found her stocking full of presents. She played with her new toys. She helped to peel the potatoes and scrubbed the carrots. Then she put on her coat and boots and went out into the garden.

Each step that Debbie took was an adventure. Slowly she walked down the path to the gate. Then she turned round and walked back, putting her feet in the footprints that she had just made. She tapped the bush by the front door and a shower of dusty snow fell onto her boots. She made a snowball and began to roll it along the ground. It got bigger and bigger. She rolled it across the grass and under her bedroom window. Then she stopped. Something shiny was sticking out of her snowball. It was a small silver sleigh bell. She rubbed it against her coat and gently shook it to and fro. A magical ringing filled the air (3). The bell seemed to be singing, 'Happy Christmas, Debbie! Happy Christmas!' Debbie smiled. She hadn't actually seen Father Christmas, but he had left her a special present; a present which had fallen from the sky on Christmas Eve.

Sound effects

1 Use hand and jingle sticks to make the sound of Father Christmas taking off. Start slowly and get faster. Fade away.

2 Sing 'Jingle bells' and accompany with hand and jingle sticks.

3 Listen to all the bells in your collection and ask the children to choose one to be the 'magic' bell. Play the bell at this point in the story.

Pass the bells round the ring

listening game

Pass the bells round the ring,
Round the ring, round the ring.
Pass the bells round the ring,
Then put them on the floor-o (shhh)

▶ Sit in a circle. Pass a set of hand jingles round the ring and sing the above words to the tune of 'Here we go round the mulberry bush'.

▶ Whoever is holding the bells when the jingle finishes tries to put the bells on the floor without making a sound. The rest of the children listen and, if they hear any jingling, put their hands on their heads. Continue in the same way.

Where's that cat?

listening game

Choose someone to be the cat. Give them a small bell to hold. Everyone else covers up their eyes. The cat creeps around the room. Every now and then it stops and rings the bell. The listening children point to where they think the sound is coming from. Be aware of children who appear to have no idea where the cat is – they may have difficulties hearing.

Creep up

listening game

Sit in a large circle with a blindfolded child in the middle and a set of hand jingles on the floor in front of him or her. Choose another child to creep up and try to take the jingles without being heard. If the blindfolded child hears the creeper and points directly at him or her, the creeper returns to the circle and another child takes his or her place

Music Box tape

listening and joining in

On Christmas Day
Join in with the repeated word endings (e.g. 'day-ay-ay-ay-ay'). Mime driving a car and playing a trumpet.

More ideas

▶ Play the singing game 'Oranges and lemons'.

▶ Play a slow descending octave on tuned percussion or keyboard from C to C to sound like church bells.

▶ Sing 'Sombody's knocking at my door' with sound effects (e.g. knocking, ringing the bell) from *Music through topics*, which contains more games and songs on the theme of bells.

Cross-curricular links

Language

▶ Encourage the children to play at being Father Christmas delivering presents, with one or two elf assistants. Use children or chairs for the reindeer. A very large box with the sides and front cut away can be the sleigh. Provide a flask and lunch box, map, chair, rug, sack of toys, reins and bells. Father Christmas gives instructions to the reindeer: go up, down, right, left, straight on, over the mountains, over the sea, faster, slower. Every so often he lands on a roof and creeps down a chimney to deliver presents.

Science

▶ Balance a broom handle across the backs of two chairs, seats facing inwards. Suspend a selection of metal objects from the pole (e.g. spoons, keys, long nails, pan lids, tin mugs, coat hangers). Put out a selection of beaters (e.g. spoons, pencils, paint brushes) and encourage the children to gently tap the metal objects. Talk about the sounds produced. What happens to the sound if you hold the metal object in your fingers while you tap it?

▶ Put out a few magnets. Ask the children to find out which of the suspended objects are magnetic.

Art and craft

▶ To make a stick jingle, cut a length of dowelling about 10 cm long. Screw a small hook in each end and attach a bell. Close the hooks using pliers. This activity is for adults, although children will enjoy watching.

▶ To make a decorative bell, spray a yoghurt pot with gold or silver paint. Make a small hole in the top using a small drill or a hot knitting needle. Decorate the bells using coloured sequins, scraps of felt or self-adhesive shapes. Dip the open end of the bell first in white glue and then in glitter. Use a pipe cleaner for a hook and tie a bow around it.

Drama

▶ Use the magic bell from the story. Pretend it can transform the children into all sorts of things. For example, ring the bell and say 'Fly like a butterfly'. The children flutter round the room until the bell stops ringing. Here are some more ideas:

> march like a soldier
> twirl like a dancer
> slither like a snake
> plod like a tortoise
> shake like a jelly
> wriggle like a worm
> bounce like a ball

▶ The movements should be as quiet as possible to allow the children to hear the magic bell.

▶ Why not link this theme with an evacuation exercise? Talk about different types of alarms (e.g. ambulance/fire engine/police sirens, fire bells, burglar and clock alarms).

Cookery

▶ Make bell-shaped biscuits and decorate them with icing and silver balls. ●

GETTING AROUND

We're driving down to London
action song

We're driving down* to London,
Can't you see?
We're driving in a motorcar
To buy a cup of tea.

We're riding down to London,
Can't you see?
We're riding in a railway train
To buy a cup of tea.

We're flying down to London,
Can't you see?
We're flying in an aeroplane
To buy a cup of tea.

We're cycling down to London,
Can't you see?
We're cycling on a bicycle
To buy a cup of tea.

We're dri-ving down to Lon-don, Can't you see?___ We're dri-ving in a mo-tor-car To buy a cup of tea.___

▶ Sit in a circle and add the following actions: steer a car, sway backwards and forwards in a railway carriage, make elbows into aeroplane wings, pedal with feet.

▶ Choose a few children for each verse to go into the middle of the circle and move around like cars, trains, aeroplanes and bicycles.

▶ Take the children outside to listen to traffic sounds. Listen to engines as they start, rev up, get faster, slow down and stop. What happens to the sound as the vehicles get nearer, go past you and then drive away into the distance? Can the children hear footsteps, people talking and shouting, birds singing, music and machinery? Make a large picture to show some of the things that you have seen and heard.

* substitute for 'up' or 'in'

Funny the way different cars start

poem about car sounds

Funny the way
Different cars start.
Some with a chunk and a jerk,
Some with a cough and a puff of smoke
Out of the back,
Some with only a little click –
with hardly any noise.

Funny the way
Different cars run.
Some rattle and bang,
Some whirr,
Some knock and knock.
Some purr
And hummmmmm
Smoothly on
with hardly any noise.

Dorothy Baruch

Traffic

game using voices to imitate traffic sounds

Invite the children, one at a time, to make the sound of a motor engine. Listen and discuss. Try to sound like a large lorry. What does a racing car sound like? Purr like a limousine.

▶ Imitate the sound of a car starting up, driving along and then stopping.

▶ Make a simple traffic light out of a circle of card – one side red, the other green. Get the vocal car engines started, then stop the traffic by showing the red light. After a few seconds turn it round to green, and so on.

▶ With older children divide the group in two, each half controlled by its own set of traffic lights.

▶ Practise car horn sounds: high, low, long, short. Make them all quite loud.

▶ Ask the children to be cars, lorries or motorbikes and to make the sounds of a busy street. The cars can decide for themselves when they stop and start. Ask the children to toot their horns 'now and then'. Tape and play back.

Coming and going

game with shakers to practise getting louder and quieter

Help each child to make an engine shaker using plasic tubs (with lids) and a variety of fillings. Buttons, coins, nails, shells and large pasta shapes make a loud sound. For smoother, quieter engine sounds use rice or sand. Don't over-fill the containers. Practise making a continuous shaking movement.

▶ Listen to the shaker engines one at a time and talk about them. Are they loud or quiet? Try playing the loud ones quietly and the quiet ones loudly.

▶ Use the shakers to make the sound of cars driving away. Start loud and get quieter. Listen to one or two of the sounds on their own. Listening children can call out 'Goodbye' and wave as the cars drive away one by one.

▶ Now make the sound of cars approaching, starting quietly and getting louder. Listening children can call out, 'Hello, nice to see you!'

▶ Show children the musical symbols for getting quieter (**>**) and getting louder (**<**).

The wheels on the bus

action song

The wheels on the bus go round and round,
Round and round,
Round and round.
The wheels on the bus go round and round,
All day long.

The engine on the bus goes brum, brum, brum . . .

The wipers on the bus go swish, swish, swish . . .

The horn on the bus goes beep, beep, beep . . .

The people on the bus go bumpety bump . . .

▶ Add actions and sounds to the song. Try to make the actions fit in with the rhythm and words.

▶ Change to a bicycle. Miss out the engine and wipers and add a bell and pedals.

What did you hear in town today?

making sounds together or in sequence

Prepare a set of six picture cards to show things that you might hear in town (e.g. car, bus, motorbike, bicycle, electric milk float, horn, bell, footsteps, people drilling, sawing and hammering on a construction site). Sit six children in a circle and put a collection of sound-makers in the middle. The collection could include plastic tub shakers, horns, bells, claves and other tappers, empty biscuit tins and beaters, scrapers and guiros.

▶ Give the children the picture cards and ask them to choose a sound-maker for their sound. They can use voices. Practise the sounds one at a time.

▶ Ask two of them to play at the *same time*. Place their cards on the floor, one directly above the other.

▶ Try three sounds together, such as hammering, sawing and drilling, or car, horn and footsteps.

▶ Try two or more sounds in *sequence*. Lay the cards in a line and stand the children in front of them. When one child stops playing, the next one starts.

Music Box tape

listening and joining in

Take you riding in my car

Join in the simple chorus. Encourage the children to clap and move to the strong, slow beat

More ideas

▶ Other well-known travelling songs include 'Yellow submarine', 'My beautiful balloon', 'Daisy, daisy' and 'Train is a-coming', all from *Knock at the door*.

▶ *This little puffin* . . . has a section called 'In the town' and includes a group of safety songs.

Cross-curricular links

Maths

▶ Paint a large picture of a double-decker bus. Make faces out of paper plates to put in the upstairs and downstairs windows. How many people are upstairs/downstairs? How many altogether? Add or take away some of the passengers and count again.

▶ Talk about trains and carriages. Get into pairs and hold each other round the waist to make trains with two carriages. Count the carriages in twos. Move around the room together. Make trains with three or four carriages. Count in threes and fours.

▶ Make a car park out of construction toys and put a few cars inside. Count the cars. Make up addition and subtraction stories. For example: 'There are three cars in the car park. Another car drives in. How many now? Two cars drive out. How many now?'

▶ Make cars out of large boxes for the children to wear (see 'Art and craft'). Line up three or more children and talk about first, second and third, or last. For example: 'What colour is the second car?'

▶ Find two toy cars of different sizes. Pass them around and ask the children to say which is the heavier/lighter. Find the answer by balancing them on scales. Can you find two toy cars that weigh the same?

▶ You will need toy lorries for this capacity game. Ask the children to guess how many bricks, conkers and bean bags they will hold. Load them up and count.

Science

▶ Use bricks and other construction toys to make a model town. Include roads, roundabouts, bridges, a railway line, tunnels, houses, flats, factories and garages. Talk about the model town using appropriate vocabulary (e.g. crossroads, junction, steep, long, narrow, straight).

▶ Test two or three similar-sized cars to see which will go the furthest when you let go of them from the top of a ramp (e.g. plank of wood). Make sure the test is fair.

▶ Find toy cars that are powered in different ways (e.g. clockwork, battery, remote control). Talk about what makes them go.

Art and craft

▶ Make and display a large frieze of a town centre. Paint roads and include a roundabout, crossroads and dead end. Print houses using large rectangular blocks (bricks) and use small squares (plastic cubes) to print windows. Sponge or hand print trees and bushes. Make colourful flower-beds with fingertip prints. Draw and cut out people and cars and stick them on the frieze. Make cars and lorries out of small cardboard boxes and fix them onto sticks. Move the stick vehicles around the town. Encourage the children to talk as they play.

▶ Make pretend cars out of large cardboard boxes for the children to wear. The
  boxes hang from the shoulders by string or rope.

Drama

▶ Pretend to be dodgem cars and drive around the room gently bumping into each
  other. Swerve, dodge and reverse.

▶ Make a zebra crossing out of paper or card and lay it across a pretend road (e.g.
  mats or skipping ropes). Talk about how to cross roads safely. Some children
  can put on the cars which they have made out of boxes and be traffic (see 'Art
  and craft'). ●

SPRING

Rain rain go away

clapping and singing rhyme

Rain rain go away,
Come again another day.

▶ Chant the rhyme slowly several times until everyone knows the words. Whisper it. Speak it loudly. Clap the rhythm as you speak (one clap per syllable). Notice that some claps are quicker than others. Quick claps are shown below by the joined-up umbrellas.

Rain,   rain,   go a - way,

Come a - gain a - no - ther day

▶ Chant and slap the rhythm on thighs. Gently tap out the rhythm on heads and chests. Try shaking the rhythm on maracas, tapping it on tambourines and woodblocks and scraping it on guiros.

▶ Sing the rhyme to the simple tune below. Accompany it by playing E and G together on the first beat of the bar all the way through (see X above the music line). Add the rhythmic accompaniment on claves or woodblocks.

Pitter patter

rhyme with rain sound effects and rhythmic chanting

Pitter patter,
Pitter patter,
Listen to the rain.
Pitter patter,
Pitter patter,
On the window pane.

▶ Learn the rhyme 'Pitter patter'. Chant it together, slowly. Keep together.

▶ Another time whisper the words 'pitter patter' over and over again to a steady beat. Ask half the group to continue with this while the rest chant the rhyme. Keep together. Encourage the children to listen to each other.

Noah

song with animal and weather sound effects

Chorus
Well the rain came down and the water rose,
It swished and it swirled round the animals' toes.
Noah said as he opened the doors,
'Stand in pairs, and wipe your paws.'

First came the ducks,   (quack quack)
Followed by the cats,   (miaow miaow)
Then came the owls,   (twit-twoo)
Followed by the rats.   (eek eek)

Chorus

Then came the sheep,   (baa baa)
Followed by the dogs,   woof woof)
Then came the snakes,   (sss sss)
Followed by the frogs.   (rabbit rabbit)

Chorus

Then came the pigs,   (snort snort)
Followed by the larks,   (tweet-tweet tweet-tweet)
Then came the ants,   (silence)
Followed by the sharks.   (swish swish)

Chorus

Then came the tigers,   (roar roar)
Cow and bull,   (moo)
'Stop!' said Noah,   (clap clap clap)
'The ark is full.'   (hip hooray)

Chorus

Well the rain came down and the water rose,
It swished and it swirled round Noah's toes.
Noah said as he closed the doors,
'I'm glad they came in twos, not fours!'

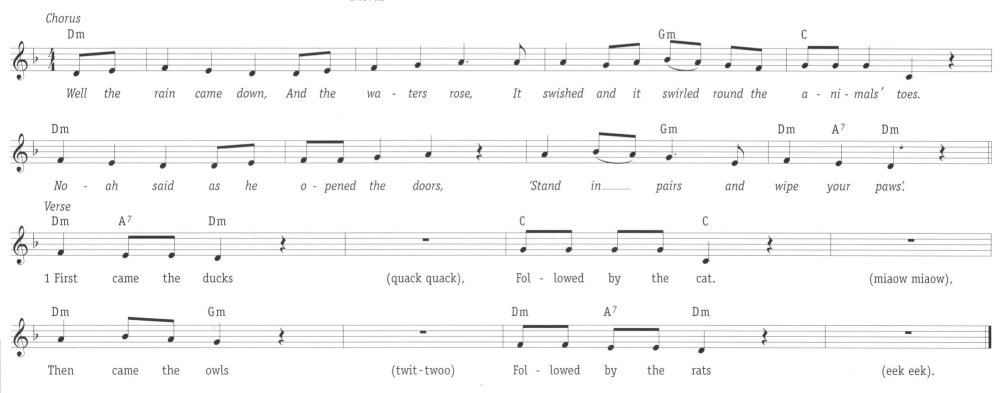

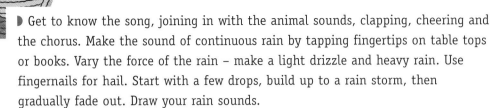

▶ Get to know the song, joining in with the animal sounds, clapping, cheering and the chorus. Make the sound of continuous rain by tapping fingertips on table tops or books. Vary the force of the rain – make a light drizzle and heavy rain. Use fingernails for hail. Start with a few drops, build up to a rain storm, then gradually fade out. Draw your rain sounds.

Animal rhythms

clapping and playing word rhythms

Chant and clap the names and rhythms of some of the animals in the ark. Remember, one clap per syllable. Say each name several times.

Make and display animal picture cards with their rhythms. Encourage the children to chant as they clap and play the rhythm. Because pig has just one clap (one syllable) it is followed by a rest symbol. This makes the rhythm sound complete and fits in better with the other animal rhythms.

▶ Older children can put two or more cards next to each other and play and chant an extended rhythm.

Animal talk

sound discrimination game

Practise making the animal sounds mentioned in the song and talk about them. Are they high or low, long or short, loud or quiet? Find instruments to imitate a hiss, snort, quack, roar, swish (shark) and squeak. Match instruments to pictures. Leave the instruments and pictures out and encourage the children to accompany themselves as they make the animal noises.

▶ Older children can draw some of the sounds on paper: high up if they are high, low if they are low; small if they are quiet, BIG if they are loud; wobbly if they are all over the place (e.g. snort), straight if they are even (e.g. squeak); short if they only last a short time (e.g. quack), long if they are drawn out (e.g. purr).

mouse

lion

pig

snake

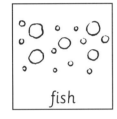

fish

cat

Animal pairs

vocal imitation of animals

One child is Noah. The rest of the children hold hands in pairs. Tell each pair which animal they are to be. Choose animals with distinctive movements and sounds. Call out 'Mix up'. The animal pairs split up and move around the room (e.g. crawling, slithering, swimming or flying) making their sound. On hearing Noah call out 'Stand in pairs!' the children get back with their partners and sit or lie in appropriate positions.

Animal get-together

listening and imitating

This is a noisy version of 'Animal pairs'. Sit in a circle. Choose five or six animals with distinctive sounds, such as a cow, lion, mouse, dog, duck or snake. Before starting the game, practise the various animal sounds and look carefully at mouth shape in relation to sound. Then walk round the circle and whisper the name of an animal to each child. Aim to have the same number of each animal. The children leave the circle and walk around the room. At a given signal they make their animal sound and look and listen for others making the same sound. Complete groups hold hands, go to the side of the room and sit down.

Music Box tape

listening and joining in

Noah
This cheerful song is printed on page 55. Join in with the animal sounds.

More ideas

▶ Sing 'The animals went in two by two' from *Apusskidu*.

▶ *Knock at the door* has a section on the rain, wind and sun.

▶ *Weather poems* by John Foster (Oxford University Press, 1993) and *This little puffin . . .* contain more weather poems and songs.

Cross-curricular links

Language

▸ Make a Noah's ark in the play corner. Use large boxes or upturned tables. Stock the ark with pairs of toy animals (e.g. two bears, two rabbits, two snakes) and feeding containers. Two or three children can pretend to be Noah and his family. They help the animals onto the ark, feed and clean them out during the voyage, look through windows at the rain, rock the boat during storms, sleep, send out the dove, cheer when it brings a leaf back and unload the boat. Improvise biblical clothing – long tunics and headdresses.

▸ Make up rhymes to describe what the animals ate on the ark: 'The pigs ate figs', 'The goats ate coats', 'The eels ate wheels.'

▸ Male and female animals have special names. Young children might know cow and bull, duck and drake, hen and cockerel.

Maths

▸ The animals came into the ark 'two by two'. Draw or stamp animal shapes on paper and ask the children to find out if they will go into twos. First count the animals and write down the number. Join the pairs. Is there an odd one out?

Science

▸ Keep a pictorial chart of the weather over a period of a week or longer.

Monday	Tuesday	Wednesday	Thursday	Friday

▸ Go out on a rainy day and see what happens to the rain when it lands on the grass, playground, road and roof. Look at gutters and drainpipes. Listen to the gurgles and splashes and drips. Where do puddles form? What happens to the water in puddles?

▸ Make a collection of waterproof clothing. Include an umbrella. Pour water over the items and see what happens. Talk about other characteristics of plastic, rubber, waxed fabrics and nylon.

▸ Take an assortment of objects from the junk box: egg box, cardboard box, foil, tissue paper, toilet roll, large screw-top lids. Ask the children which ones they think are waterproof. Test. Identify the materials from which they are made.

▸ Make waterproof shelters for toys using cardboard boxes. Experiment to find different ways of making the boxes waterproof. For example, try rubbing them with wax crayons or candles, or covering them with PVA glue or plastic shopping bags.

Art and craft

▸ Make a large picture of Noah and his ark. Paint a huge rainbow at the back. Make the sun out of gold paper and print slanting rain using the side of a ruler. Paint and cut out the ark separately and stick it on so that it bulges in the middle, giving a 3-D effect. Include the heads of the animals – coming out of roofs, port holes and doors and looking over the edge of the ark.

▸ Talk about and paint animals with stripes, such as zebras, snakes and tigers. Paint some spotted creatures, such as leopards, dalmatians and fish. Print the stripes and spots.

▸ Paint a picture on the top half of a sheet of paper. Fold the bottom half over the wet paint to make a reflection picture.

Drama

▸ The *Carnival of animals* by Saint Saens includes passages of music which young children find appealing. Dart and dive to 'The aquarium', tread slowly to 'The elephant', glide along to 'The swan' and prowl to 'The lion'.

▸ Get in animal pairs and move into a pretend ark. The snakes slide on their bellies and hiss; the tigers prowl and snarl; the monkeys dance and gibber; the parrots fly and screech. Can each pair move identically and keep together? Let Noah announce each animal duo. ●

The little red hen

traditional story with sound effects and chanted or sung responses

A little red hen lived in a cottage with a rat, a dog and a cat. The rat, the dog and the cat were lazy animals, but the little red hen was busy from dawn till dusk. One day she decided to sow some seeds of corn. She needed help with the weeding and digging, so she said to the rat:

'Rat, Rat, Please will you help me?'

Rat was very comfortable lying in a hammock in the Spring sunshine. He replied:

'No not I.'

The little red hen went over to the dog asleep in front of the fire. She said:

'Dog, Dog, Please will you help me?'

Dog didn't even look up. He said:

'No not I.'

The little red hen wasn't very pleased. She looked around for Cat and spotted her snoozing on the end of the bed. She said:

'Cat, Cat, Please will you help me?'

Cat opened one eye and yawned. She flicked the end of her tail and said:

'No not I.'

'Hoity toity,' said the little red hen to herself, and she rolled up her sleeves and set to work. She pulled out the weeds and she dug over the soil and she raked out the lumps (1). The sun was setting as she scattered the last of the corn seeds on the soil (2).

The sun shone and the rain fell and the seeds in the ground began to grow. First the pointed green shoots appeared, then the stalks and leaves, and finally the ears of corn (3). The corn turned from green to golden brown, and one dry sunny day the little red hen decided it was time to cut it all down and gather in her harvest of corn seed.

She said to the rat:

'Rat, Rat, Please will you help me?'

The rat was on the roof of the shed enjoying the last of the summer sun. He twitched his whiskers and said:

'No not I.'

The little red hen bustled over to the dog who was on the back doorstep dreaming about rabbits. She said :

'Dog, Dog, Please will you help me?'

The dog didn't want to interrupt his dream so he murmured:

'No not I.'

Cat was on a cushion washing herself. The little red hen flapped her wings to get her attention and said:

'Cat,   Cat,   Please will you help me?'

With one leg still stuck up in the air, Cat said:

'No not I.'

'Hoity toity,' said the little red hen to herself, and she went off to get the scythe. Up and down the field went the little red hen cutting down the dry corn stalks (4). By the time she had stacked up the corn and carried it back to the shed it was dark.

The little red hen wanted to use the corn to make some bread. But first she had to take the grain to the mill to be ground into flour. The sacks of corn seed were heavy. She went into the cottage where all three animals were snoozing on the settee and said:

'Rat,   Rat,   Please will you help me?'

'Dog,   Dog,   Please will you help me?'

'Cat,   Cat,   Please will you help me?'

All three animals answered together:

'No not I.'

'Hoity toity, hoity toity, hoity toity,' said the little red hen. She loaded one of the sacks onto a wheelbarrow and trudged up the hill to the mill. There the jolly miller ground her seeds of corn into fine, white flour (5).

Back home the little red hen stoked up the fire, put on her pinafore and started to mix the flour with water, yeast and salt to make the bread dough. Several hours later the delicious smell of baking wafted through the house. The three lazy animals opened their eyes, lifted up their heads and sniffed. They watched the little red hen as she took the crusty loaves out of the oven and tipped them out of their tins to cool. Their mouths began to water. They got up and said:

'Hen,   Hen,   Please can we have some?'

The little red hen packed the loaves into a basket and put on her scarf. As she marched out of the cottage she said, firmly:

'NO YOU CAN'T.'

▶ Read the story and then talk about it. Why wouldn't the animals help? How do you think the little red hen felt when she had to do all the work herself? Where do you think she was going at the end of the story?

▶ Encourage the children to join in chanting or singing the animals' questions and answers.

Sound effects

▶ Choose a percussion instrument for each lazy animal – one for the rat, one for the dog and one for the cat. Use the instruments to accompany the rhythm of 'No not I', which should be sleepy and quiet. When all three animals speak together, play all three instruments.

▶ Add sound effects for digging, raking, sowing the seeds, the growing corn, cutting the corn and grinding the corn (see numbers in text). Talk about each situation and experiment with different instruments until you find an appropriate sound effect.

Hickety pickety my black hen

rhyme for rhythmic chanting

    X   *X*   *X*   *X*
Hickety pickety my black hen,

   X   *X*   *X*   *X*
She lays eggs for gentlemen.

   X   *X*   *X*   *X*
Sometimes nine and sometimes ten,

   X   *X*   *X*   *X*
Hickety pickety my black hen.

▶ Chant the rhyme several times, until the children are joining in. Keep the tempo slow and tap the beat (see X above the rhyme) on your thighs. Invite a child with a good sense of time to tap the beat on a tambourine or claves.

▶ Write '9' on one side of a card and '10' on the other. At the end of the rhyme turn one side of the card towards the children. Lead them in clapping and counting until they reach the number displayed. One or two children can accompany the counting with instruments.

Humpty Dumpty

nursery rhyme with sound effects

Humpty Dumpty sat on a wall.
Humpty Dumpty had a great fall.
All the King's horses and all the King's men
Couldn't put Humpty together again.

▶ Tap chime bars or rub the bars of a xylophone/glockenspiel from high to low (short to long) to describe Humpty falling off the wall. Give him a crash-landing. Pause at the end of the second line to make the sound of the approaching soldiers. Use claves, woodblocks, coconut shells or pairs of yoghurt pots for galloping hoofs. Get louder to suggest getting nearer. At the end the soldiers can ride off again. Get quieter to suggest moving into the distance.

Five warm eggs in an incubator

counting song with percussion accompaniment

Five warm eggs in an incubator,
Tipper tipper tap, and a little bit later
Broken shell in the incubator,
One damp chicken on the floor.

Four warm eggs in an incubator
Tipper tipper tap, and a little bit later
Broken shell in the incubator,
Two damp chickens on the floor.

▶ Continue until there are five hatched chickens and no eggs in the incubator. Finish with a lot of high-pitched peeping sounds.

▶ It helps with the counting if you act out the song. You will need an incubator (mat), a light (child standing up) and five eggs (children curled up small).

▶ On 'Tipper tipper tap' touch one of the eggs. The chosen egg breaks and out comes a chicken (tuck hands under armpits for wings and walk in a crouched position). The chick wobbles off the mat to the light, where it rests and dries its feathers. Continue until all the eggs have hatched.

▶ When the children know the song, ask them to clap (tap) the rhythm to 'Tipper tipper tap'. Gently tap a cymbal or triangle on the first word of the last line of each verse (e.g. 'one', 'two', 'three').

▶ Older children can try the simple xylophone accompaniment (see music). Any tuned instrument will do.

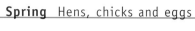

Music Box tape

listening and joining in

Old MacDonald had a farm

Listen to the song and talk about the animals mentioned: cows, ducks, donkey, pigs, hens. Imitate their sounds. Sing the song adding your own animals and machines. Keep the speed slow.

More ideas

▶ There is a section on hens and chicks in *Music through topics*. It includes a story called 'The fabulous egg', as well as poems, songs, games and ideas for listening.

▶ *This little puffin* . . . has a section on farms, which includes several traditional songs and poems.

Cross-curricular links

Language

▸ Make up and act out a story on the theme of non-cooperation based on the story of the little red hen. You need someone who is trying to get a job done and two or three people who won't help because they are lazy. First think of a job that needs doing: tidying the play corner, putting the bricks away, washing the paint brushes. Make up questions and replies. Match gestures and vocal expression to the meaning of the words. Give the stories happy endings.

▸ Find words that rhyme with hen, rat, dog, cat and fox. Make up simple rhymes: 'The dog sniffed the frog.' Make sets of the rhyming words using picture/word cards.

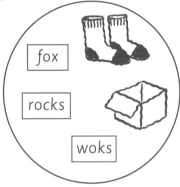

▸ The little red hen had to go to a lot of trouble to get her bread. What would she have to do if she wanted a new pullover, butter on her bread or a new table? Remember, she can't just pop to the shop!

Maths

▸ Make a collection of eggs (e.g. hard-boiled, tin, cardboard, wooden). Talk about their shape (round, curved). What's the difference between a ball shape (sphere) and an egg shape (ovoid)? Roll both shapes. Can you make eggs roll in a straight line? Why not?

▸ Put five eggs on a plate. Ask the children to close their eyes. Remove one or more eggs. Ask the children to open their eyes and say how many eggs have been taken. This game helps to establish simple number bonds. Older children could start with more eggs, very young children with less.

▸ Make up number stories about Easter eggs: 'Sam had five eggs. He ate two. How many are left?' or 'Vikki had two eggs. Her auntie gave her another. How many altogether?'

Science

▸ Make bread. What happens when you mix the yeast with sugar and warm water? What happens if you miss out the sugar? Will the yeast react to cold water?

▸ Make scrambled egg on toast. Break an egg into a glass bowl and look at it carefully. Talk about its structure (yolk and white), colour, smell and texture. Beat the egg and add seasoning. Cook. Look at the colour and texture of the cooked egg. Put on toast and eat.

▸ Make egg sandwiches. Use a timer and boil an egg. Cool the egg under cold water and peel off the shell. Compare the appearance and texture of the boiled egg to that of the raw egg. Mash up with seasoning and mayonnaise or salad cream. Spread on bread, make into sandwiches and eat.

▸ Scatter some corn seeds on a plate covered with several layers of damp kitchen tissue. Watch the corn grow and record the growth on a chart. Try growing corn seeds on dry kitchen paper or on damp kitchen tissue in a dark box. What happens?

▸ Try growing corn seeds on clay or in soil, sawdust, water or sand. Keep all the substances moist and in the light.

Art and craft

▸ Make a giant Humpty Dumpty by stuffing a pillowcase with paper. Give him a face, hair, arms and legs (stuffed tights). Dress him in real clothes. Build a wall out of shoe boxes. Try to copy a brick wall pattern.

▸ Grow cress in empty egg shells. Blow eggs and break off the shell around the top. Carefully draw a face on the shell with felt-tips. Stuff cotton wool in the hole and dampen. Sprinkle cress seeds over the cotton wool and wait for the 'hair' to grow. Keep the wool damp. ●

Jack and the beanstalk

traditional story with sound effects

Jack and his widowed mother are experiencing hard times. Jack is sent to market to sell Daisy the cow. On the way he meets a curious old man who gives him magic beans in exchange for Daisy. Jack is thrilled, but his mother is not. She tosses the beans out of the window and sends Jack to bed.

In the night a huge beanstalk grows. On waking, Jack sees the beanstalk and climbs up it. At the top is a strange land strewn with boulders and he sets off towards a distant castle. When he gets there, he knocks on the huge door. A woman opens it and tells him to go away or he will be eaten up by her husband the giant. Jack, however, is hungry and slips into the kitchen.

The giant approaches and Jack hides. The giant shouts 'FEE FI FO FUM!', and after a hearty meal falls asleep while counting his gold. Jack steals the gold and runs for his life. He is chased but manages to escape down the beanstalk.

Back home his mum is delighted with the gold. When it runs out, Jack climbs the beanstalk once again. This time he takes a singing harp. On his third visit to the castle he runs off with a hen that lays golden eggs. This time the giant climbs down the beanstalk after Jack and nearly catches him. Jack's mother chops away at the stalk and the giant topples down to the ground, dead. Jack and his mum live in idle luxury for the rest of their lives.

▶ Tell the story of Jack and the beanstalk – from memory, if possible. The above summary may be helpful.

Sound effects

▶ Chant the following phrases, using appropriate vocal expression and volume:

    poor old cow – *slow and sad*

    magic beans – *high and excited*

    naughty little boy – *staccato and cross*

    FEE FI FO FUM – *slow and deep and loud*

▶ Incorporate *body* and *vocal* sound effects into the story. Encourage everyone to join in:

    mouth clicks for the cow's hoofs

    rising hum for growth of beanstalk

    slow stamps on spot for the giant's footsteps

    clucking sounds for hen

    slapped thighs for Jack's running feet

    loud claps for chopping axe

    descending hum for toppling beanstalk, with crashing sound at the end

▶ Another time add *instrumental* sound effects. At first practise the sounds in isolation. Later incorporate them into the story.

Experiment to find a sound for the cow's hoofs on the road. Can you make it sound as though the cow is disappearing into the distance?

Make a rattling sound for the beans.

Make up quiet magic music to describe the beanstalk growing up into the sky. Collect as many ringing and chiming instruments as possible.

Stand a glockenspiel or xylophone on its wide end and support firmly. Tap each bar from bottom (longest note) to top (shortest bar) to describe Jack climbing the beanstalk. Slow down as he reaches the top to show that he is getting tired.

To descend the beanstalk start with the shortest bar and play quickly down towards the floor. End with a crash (e.g. cymbals, drum, tambourine).

Find sounds for the giant's footsteps, gold, harp, hen and axe. Think about speed and volume.

Up and down the beanstalk

game practising getting higher and getting lower

▶ Sing the two phrases and imitate the direction of the tune by standing up and sitting down.

▶ Play the tunes on a pitched percussion instrument or keyboard (no words). Ask the children to use their fingers to 'do what the tune says'. If it goes up, point upwards; if it goes down, touch the floor.

▶ Paint a beanstalk about a metre high. Display it so that its base is at ground level. Choose a toy to represent Jack. Invite a child to either play up or down the glockenspiel or keyboard. Ask another child to make Jack do what the music says, i.e. climb up or down the painted beanstalk. Think about speed.

Oats and beans and barley grow

action rhyme

Oats and beans and barley grow,
Oats and beans and barley grow,
Do you or I or anyone know
How oats and beans and barley grow?

▶ What makes things grow? Ask the children for their ideas.

▶ Chant the rhyme 'Oats and beans and barley grow'. In line three point (with both forefingers) to a friend on 'you' and to your own chest on 'I'. On 'anyone' spread both hands out in front as though asking a question.

▶ Clap or slap (on thighs) the beat in lines one, two and four.

I had a little cherry stone

action rhyme with pretend stone

I had a little cherry stone,   *(hold stone with thumb and forefinger)*
I put it in the ground.   *(push stone into hole made by other hand)*
And when next year I went to look
A little shoot I found.   *(push tip of forefinger up through hole)*

The shoot grew upwards day by day   *(move finger upwards)*
And soon became a tree.   *(spread arms out to make tree shape)*
I picked the juicy cherries   *(mime picking cherries)*
And I ate them for my tea.   *(mime eating cherry; spit out stone and get*
                                             ready to plant it)

▶ Collect some pips, seeds and stones and talk about them. Soak for a day, then plant in soil. Watch them grow.

▶ How long does it take for a tree to grow? If you planted a cherry stone today, how long would it be before you could pick its cherries: a day, a week, a year or longer?

▶ Chant the poem with new words:

I had a little apple pip . . .
I had a little orange pip . . .
I had a little grape seed . . .
I had a hairy mango stone . . .

Shake it all about

sound discrimination game

 Use seed shakers (see 'Art and craft') for this game. Ask the children to listen to and then copy a shaking sound. Was it loud or quiet, long or short? Try getting louder or quieter. Draw the sounds.

short   long   loud and short

Guess the filling

sound discrimination game

 Fill three identical containers (e.g. margarine tubs) with three different types of seeds (e.g. cress, rice, beans). Listen to each in turn. Talk about the sounds. Guess the fillings.

Music Box tape

listening and joining in

Dig, dig, dig
The little red hen had to work hard to grow her corn seeds. This song describes digging, raking and hoeing. Mime the three actions: dig with a steady, strong downwards movement of hands and feet; slowly push and pull an imaginary rake to and fro; hoe with short, quick jabbing movements. Accompany the chorus with body sounds: three stamps on 'dig, dig, dig', three thigh slaps on 'rake, rake, rake' and three claps for 'hoe, hoe, hoe'. Note the pattern: stamp, slap, stamp, clap.

More ideas

▶ The section called 'Higher and lower' in *High low dolly pepper* is relevant to this unit.

▶ You will find the songs 'One man went to mow' and 'I went to the garden' in *This little puffin . . .*

Cross-curricular links

Language

▶ Paint the words 'beans' and 'rice' using lots of glue. Stick the appropriate seeds over the words.

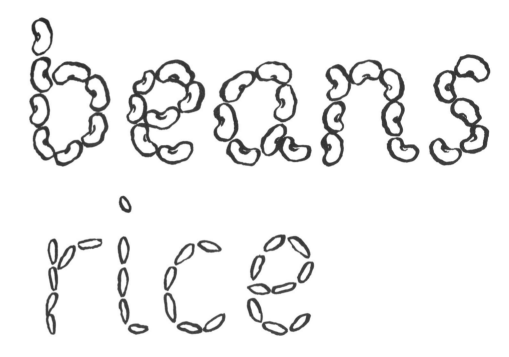

▶ Make up a story together called 'Jane and the peastalk'. How did Jane get the peas? What was at the top of the stalk?

Maths

▶ Bring in pea pods. Give a pod to each child and count the peas. Who has the least, the same, the most? Eat the peas one at a time, re-counting the peas as you go.

Science

▶ Grow broad beans in jam jars or small milk bottles. Slide the beans between kitchen paper and the glass so they can be seen. Keep the paper damp. Watch for changes.

▶ Grow beans in soil in yoghurt pots. Watch out for the shoot. Use cubes to measure the stalk as it grows.

Art and craft

▶ Help the children to make their own seed shakers using a variety of containers (no glass jars) and seeds, such as rice, melon seeds, lentils, beans and avocado stones. Make sure the containers are small enough for small hands to hold and that the lids can be firmly attached to the base. Vary the quantity of seeds in the shakers. Do not overfill. Decorate with paint or self-adhesive shapes.

▶ Shake the seed shakers, listen to them and describe the sounds (e.g. fizzy, rattly, soft, clunky). Encourage comparisons, such as 'sounds like rain', 'sounds like clapping' or 'sounds like machinery'. Move to the sounds. Use the shakers to make sound effects for stories, poems and songs.

▶ Make a huge beanstalk stretching from floor to ceiling. Twist crepe paper for the stalk. Cut leaves out of sugar paper and draw veins on them. Use crumpled orange tissue paper for flowers. For the bean pods use painted kitchen roll tubes or staple together two bean-shaped pieces of paper and stuff with newspaper. Use junk material to make Jack (small) and the giant (big) and fix them to the beanstalk.

▶ Make seed pictures/patterns. Be generous with the glue.

Drama

▶ Act out parts of the story of Jack and the beanstalk. Add some of the sound effects practised earlier. The suggestions below may be helpful.

> Walk slowly and sadly along a pretend road in pairs (Jack and the cow).

> Act out Jack's mum being cross with her son. One person is the mum, who throws the seeds out of the window. Jack can stomp upstairs to bed.

> Make up movements to suggest magic.

> Pretend to climb the beanstalk, then look around in wonder at the strange land.

> Pretend to be Jack creeping about the giant's kitchen. Run and hide each time you hear the giant's footsteps.

> In pairs (giant and Jack) chase round the room. The giants take long strides, the Jacks take short, quick steps.

▶ Pretend to be jumping beans (jump with two feet together), runner beans (run lightly on toes), baked beans (get into fours and squash together in a tin), French beans (say *bonjour* to each other), broad beans (look fat) and old beans (walk slowly with bent knees).

Cookery

▶ Make a vegetable curry or rice pudding. Look carefully at the rice before and after cooking. Note the change in taste, texture, size and colour.

▶ Make a mixed bean salad.

▶ Make baked beans on toast. ●

The gingerbread man

traditional story

An old woman was making gingerbread biscuits. She used the bits of dough left over to make a little gingerbread man. She cut out his head, his tummy and his arms and legs, gave him two currant eyes and an orange peel mouth and popped him in the oven.

A few minutes later she heard a voice calling from the oven: 'Let me out! Let me out!' She opened the oven door and out jumped a hot little gingerbread man. He ran out of the door.

'STOP!' shouted the woman. 'Come back!'

But the gingerbread man shook his head. He ran on, and as he ran he sang:

Run, run, as fast as you can, You can't catch me I'm the gin - ger - bread man.

'Run, run, as fast as you can,
You can't catch me, I'm the gingerbread man.'

The old woman couldn't keep up with the gingerbread man so she went back home to take the rest of her biscuits out of the oven before they burnt.

On down the road ran the gingerbread man, glad to be out of the hot oven and in the fresh air. He came to a field of cows. One of the cows was very interested to see him running by.

'MOO!' she said. 'Wait for me.'
But the gingerbread man shook his head. He ran on, and as he ran he sang:
'Run, run, as fast as you can,
You can't catch me, I'm the gingerbread man.'

A billy goat was eating grass by the side of the road. He was surprised to see the little brown gingerbread man bowling up the road towards him. As the gingerbread man ran by he bleated, 'MEH-EH-EH-EH-EH! Can I come with you?'

But the gingerbread man shook his head. He ran on, and as he ran he sang:
'Run, run, as fast as you can,
You can't catch me, I'm the gingerbread man.'

The gingerbread man came to a crossroads where a horse and cart was standing. The horse was tired of pulling cartloads of hay and he shook his head and snorted as the gingerbread man ran by.

'BRRRRRRR! Jump in my cart and we'll run away together,' he snorted.

But the gingerbread man shook his head. He ran on, and as he ran he sang:
'Run, run, as fast as you can,
You can't catch me, I'm the gingerbread man.'

The gingerbread man's feet were beginning to get tired of running along the hard, dusty road. He ran through a hedge and into a field. He liked the feel of the soft, cool grass. At the end of the field was a river, and, sitting on the bank of the river, was a sleek red fox.

'Good morning,' said the fox. 'And what can I do for you?'

The gingerbread man stopped. He wasn't sure what to do next. There was no bridge and he wanted to cross the river.

'Perhaps you would allow me to carry you across this deep, cold and very wide river,' said the sly fox. 'Sit on my back. You'll be quite safe there.'

The gingerbread man jumped up onto the fox's shiny red fur. The fox waded into the river and began to swim. The gingerbread man felt his toes getting wet.

'Climb up on my neck,' purred the fox. 'You'll be quite safe there.'

So the gingerbread man pulled himself up the fox's neck and held onto his ears.

'Would you mind moving onto my nose?' said the fox. 'You're hurting my ears.'

Slowly the gingerbread man climbed over the fox's head and perched on the long, pointy nose of the fox.

'Comfortable?' murmured the fox.

'Yes thank you,' said the gingerbread man.

'Good,' said the fox. And with one quick flick of his head he tossed the gingerbread man up in the air, opened his mouth and SNAP, the gingerbread man disappeared down his mouth.

▶ Encourage the children to join in the repeated chorus. The tune resembles the last two lines of 'Here we go round the mulberry bush'. Lightly tap a slow beat on thighs to keep the singing together. Add vocal sound effects for the animal sounds and clap hands together with a SNAP at the end.

▶ Make a huge picture showing the route taken by the gingerbread man from the oven to the fox's nose (see 'Art and craft'). Tell the story in sound, without words. Control the sequence of sound by moving a pointer along the road and across the field. Tap a tambour to describe the sound of the running gingerbread man. Produce a softer sound as the gingerbread man runs across the field. Add animal sounds. For the flowing water of the river, rub beaters quietly up and down an instrument with metal bars. Finish with a loud SNAP (e.g. claves or ruler slapped on table).

Bubble bubble bubble

rhyme with a strong beat

    x   x
Bubble, said the kettle,

    x   x
Bubble, said the pot,

    x   x
Bubble, bubble, bubble,

   x   x
We are very, very hot.

▶ Chant the rhyme a few times until most of the children are joining in. Keep the tempo slow. Emphasise the slow beat (see X above the rhyme).

▶ Divide the group into two. One group chants the first line. The other chants the second line. Both groups chant lines three and four together.

▶ Chant the rhyme against a bubbling accompaniment made by voices, instruments and water sounds (e.g. blow down a straw).

Polly put the kettle on

song for two groups of children

Polly put the kettle on,   Sukey take it off again,
Polly put the kettle on,   Sukey take it off again,
Polly put the kettle on   Sukey take it off again
We'll all have tea.   They've all gone away.

▶ This nursery rhyme has two distinct tunes – Sukey's and Polly's. First, sing the whole song through several times, until most children know it well. Then split the group into two. One group is Sukey telling Polly to put the kettle on; the other is Polly telling Sukey to take it off.

▶ Act out the rhyme with Polly and Sukey, a few children as visitors and some domestic props. Encourage solo singing. Change the names to include boys. For ease of singing, stick to names with two syllables (e.g. Si-mon, Dar-ren).

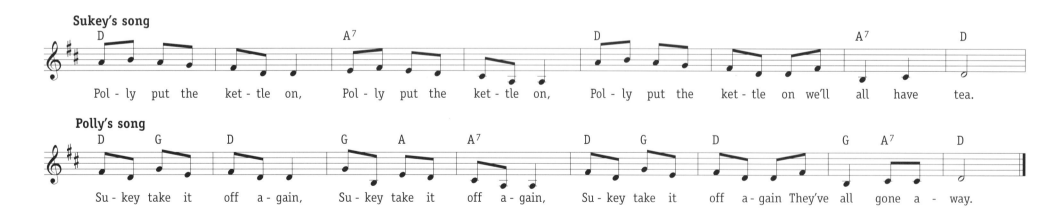

Kitchen sounds

experimenting with sound

 Collect kitchen utensils which make interesting sounds, such as whisks, cheese graters, wooden spoons, pan lids, baking trays, cooling trays and spoons. Put them in the middle of a circle and let the children experiment with them to make interesting sounds. Use the spoons as beaters on pans and as scrapers on graters and wire trays. Describe the sounds.

What's cooking?

sound discrimination game

 Choose two distinctive kitchen sounds (e.g. whisk and grater). Make a screen with an up-ended table. Go behind the screen and make one of the sounds. Ask the children to identify it. Increase the number of sounds to three then four. The children can play this game on their own.

Sound sandwiches

patterns of sound made with kitchen utensils

 Sit in a circle. Give half the children two spoons each. Practise tapping them together. Point to the spoon players when you want them to play and make a sign when you want them to stop. Give the other children kitchen equipment with which to make different sounds (see above). Listen to each in turn using agreed starting and stopping gestures.

▶ Explain to the children that you are going to make some sound sandwiches. Each sandwich is made out of two pieces of bread (sound made by spoons) and a filling (another sound).

▶ Start with a piece of bread. Point to the spoon players and let them tap for a few seconds. Stop them with a gesture and point to one of the other kitchen sounds. After a few seconds turn to the spoons again. There should be no spoken instructions. You will need to play this game several times until it flows smoothly. Make lots of sandwiches with lots of different fillings.

Rice and tuna

echo song

 Rice and tuna,
Rice and tuna, *(echo)*
Beans on toast,
Beans on toast, *(echo)*
Pizza and spaghetti,
Pizza and spaghetti, *(echo)*
Pancake roll,
Pancake roll. *(echo)*

▶ Sing the song to the tune of 'Frère Jacques'. Teach it as an echo song: the leader sings line one and the children echo with line two, and so on. Keep the pace slow. Older children can make up their own versions.

Music Box tape

listening and joining in

 Jelly on the plate
Listen to the words and accompanying sound effects: wobbling jelly, sloppy custard, crumbly biscuits. Make up some more food verses, such as 'toffee in my mouth' or 'cornflakes in a bowl'.

More ideas

▶ Sing 'Pease pudding hot' and 'I'm a little teapot' from *Knock at the door*.

▶ Sing 'Ten fat sausages' from *Okki-tokki-unga*.

▶ Sing 'Crash! Bang! Ouch! And whoops-a-daisy' from *Music through topics*.

▶ Read 'No peace for Hammy' from *Music through topics*, adding sound effects.

▶ Read *Stone soup* by Tony Ross (Picture Lions, 1995).

▶ Read *The tiger who came to tea* by Judith Kerr (Picture Lions, 1991).

Cross-curricular links

Language

▶ Make the play corner into a café or tearoom. Include a range of kitchen equipment and pretend cakes, biscuits and drinks. Make and display a simple menu. Keep the prices low (e.g. 1p, 2p, 5p). Give the customers real money to pay for the food. Make signs: 'Open', 'Closed', 'Wheelchairs welcome', 'No smoking'.

▶ Make your own soup (e.g. Playgroup soup, Nursery soup, Class One soup). You will need a large container – a bucket will do. Sit in a circle with the pot in the middle. Ask each child to put one thing from the room into the soup. In turn the children hold up their 'ingredient' and say what it is before placing it in the pot. At the end, stir the soup with a large spoon, pretend to taste it and pronounce it delicious. Older children can use a describing word for their item (e.g. a *red* cube, a *long* piece of string, an *old* paint apron, a *small* piece of plasticine).

Maths

▶ Put out three or four spoons. Ask the children to put them in order, starting with the longest/shortest.

▶ Put out a set of scales and various pairs of objects: 2 spoons, 2 pans, 2 potatoes, 2 boxes of cereal. Check that the pans are balanced. Encourage the children to use the scales to find out which is the lighter/heavier object of the pair.

▶ Bring in a kitchen timer. Can the children sit still for one minute? How many times can they write their name in a minute? Put out several games and jigsaws and choose a child for each. Let them play for five minutes – use the timer. When the bell goes, everyone moves on one game.

▶ Use money to buy food and drink in the café (see 'Language').

▶ Use cutters to make different biscuit shapes: round, square, triangular. Decorate with blobs of icing in each corner of the biscuit.

Art and craft

▶ Make a large map to show the travels of the gingerbread man. Paint in the road, the fields and the river. Print bushes and hedges. Make trees by scrunching up large pieces of tissue paper. Use a painted box for the cottage.

▶ Make the old woman and the animals out of toilet rolls and stick them in the appropriate places on the map. Make the gingerbread man out of stiff card and mount him on a stick. Move him around in front of the map as you tell the story.

▶ Make large symmetrical gingerbread men and women. Fold a large piece of paper in half vertically and draw half the figure. Cut round the shape and open out. Paint and decorate with bits and pieces.

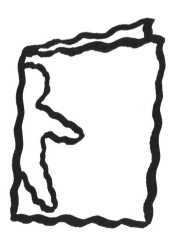

Drama

▶ Ask the children, one at a time, to pretend to do a job in the kitchen, such as ironing, stirring, breaking eggs, cutting bread, peeling potatoes, brushing the floor, washing up and filling the kettle. Ask the other children to guess what they are doing.

▶ Sing the following to the tune of 'Here we go round the mulberry bush' with appropriate actions. Add more verses.

> This is the way we iron the clothes
> Iron the clothes, iron the clothes
> This is the way we iron the clothes
> When we're in the kitchen.
>
> This is the way we wash the pans . . .
>
> This is the way we beat an egg . . .

Cookery

▶ Make gingerbread men and women. What happens to the colour and texture of the dough when it is cooked? Pretend to be foxes and eat the gingerbread men and women up. ●

SUMMER

PRINCES AND PRINCESSES

There was a princess long ago

singing and dancing game

1 There was a princess long ago,
Long ago, long ago.
There was a princess long ago,
Long, long ago.

2 And she lived in a big, high tower,
A big, high tower, a big, high tower,
And she lived in a big, high tower,
Long, long ago.

3 A wicked fairy cast a spell . . .

4 The princess slept for a hundred years . . .

5 A great big forest grew around . . .

6 A brave young prince came riding by . . .

7 He chopped those trees down one by one . . .

8 He knelt and woke the fair princess . . .

9 So everybody's happy now . . . *(sing twice)*

Actions

VERSE 1
Walk round in a circle holding hands. The princess sits on a cushion in the middle.

VERSE 2
Stop walking and raise joined hands to make the high tower.

VERSE 3
The wicked fairy pushes into the ring and dances around the frightened princess, waving a stick.

VERSE 4
The princess curls up and goes to sleep on the cushion.

VERSE 5
Children in the circle wave their arms in the air like trees.

VERSE 6
The prince gallops round the outside of the circle.

VERSE 7
The prince dismounts and walks round the outside of the circle touching the children one by one on their shoulders. The 'trees' topple to the ground.

VERSE 8
The prince kneels by the princess and wakes her up.

VERSE 9
The prince and princess join hands. The rest of the children get into circles of two or three. Everyone dances round singing. Repeat the last verse.

Sound effects

▶ When you know the song well, find sounds to represent magic, horses' hooves and trees being chopped down.

Magic

matching instrumental sounds to moods

 Sit in a large circle and place a selection of musical instruments (plus beaters) and other sound-makers in the centre. Ask half the children to choose an instrument each and to make magic music. The purpose of the magic is to make the rest of the children feel sleepy. Listen to each sound in turn. At the end, ask the listeners if the magic worked. Did it make them want to close their eyes and go to sleep? Talk about some of the sounds. Swap over and let the listeners have a go.

▶ Another time make some magic *happy* music. Talk about the volume, speed and rhythm of the sounds. Did the music make the children get up and dance around and clap their hands?

▶ Can the children make creepy, angry, sad and crazy music? Encourage the non-players to show how the music made them feel through facial expressions and actions.

Abracadabra

chanting and clapping word rhythms

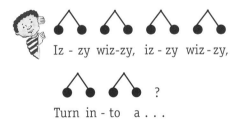

Iz - zy wiz-zy, iz - zy wiz-zy,

Turn in - to a . . .

▶ Stand in a circle. Practise chanting and clapping the rhythm of the spell below. Give one of the children an easy-to-play instrument (e.g. small tambourine or claves) and ask him or her to chant and tap the rhythm of a spell. Make up an ending (e.g. 'Turn into a tree'). The listening children are magicked into whatever is named. Pass the instrument to another child for another spell.

▶ Make up some new spells with different rhythms. Here are two ideas:

Hun-ky dor - y, jack - a - nor - y,

Turn in - to a . . . ?

Did-dle did-dle dum-pling,

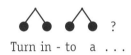

Turn in - to a . . . ?

Up and down the tower

game practising getting higher and getting lower

 You will need a medium-sized xylophone or glockenspiel for this game. Remove some of the small (top) bars, leaving the first eight notes (C D E F G A B C) in place. Support the instrument in an upright position, with the longest (lowest) bars near the floor.

▶ Tell the children that you are going to make the sound of the princess climbing up the high tower to her little room at the top. Tap the bars slowly, one at a time, starting with the lowest note (longest bar). Then play her going down the steps.

▶ Repeat, but this time ask the children to move their hands up or down in the air as you play. Vary the speed (e.g. 'Now she's climbing the stairs slowly', 'Now she's running down the stairs').

▶ Another time ask the children to listen to the music and to tell you whether the princess is going up or down the stairs. Play either up or down the notes. When you have the right answer, play it again and ask the children to move their hands up or down. This repetition helps to reinforce listening skills.

▶ Older children can try to identify a wider range of sounds: the highest note repeated means she is staying upstairs; the lowest note repeated means she is staying downstairs.

▶ Can the children describe what the princess is doing with their eyes closed? Some children will find this difficult.

▶ Make up short stories about the princess in the tower and use the tuned percussion to describe her movements. For example: 'The princess didn't want to go to bed. She walked slowly upstairs', 'The princess heard her mother calling and ran quickly dowstairs', 'The princess went halfway upstairs then went back down to get her teddy, 'The princess went halfway upstairs, sat and had a rest for a few seconds, then carried on up to the top.'

▶ When the children are good at telling the difference between getting higher and getting lower, play the game with the instrument in its usual horizontal position.

Ride a horse to town

rhyme with rhythmic actions

     x   *x*   *x*   *x*
Ride a horse, ride a horse,

     x   *x*   *x*
Ride a horse to town.

     x   *x* *x*   *x*
Ride a horse, ride a horse,

          x   *x*
WHOOPS! Fall down.

▶ Bob up and down in time with the chanting. On 'WHOOPS!', throw hands into the air and topple to the ground.

▶ Listen to several instruments (e.g. tambourine, tambour, woodblock, maracas, claves, jingles bells, triangle) and keep out those which make the children think of horses' hooves. Coconut shells sound good, but they are usually too large to be held by young children. Two small yoghurt pots tapped together at the open end sound realistic.

▶ Use the selected instruments to make hoof noises to fit in with the beat of the rhyme (see X above the rhyme). Stop at the end of line three. Non-players clap twice, loudly, in time with the words 'fall down'.

▶ Ask the children, one at a time, to make some of the following horse sound effects using mouth clicks, instruments or yoghurt pots:

> trotting (steady, regular sound, like a clock)
> galloping (fast, skipping rhythm: de-DUM de-DUM)
> a horse trotting away (regular sound getting quieter)
> a horse galloping towards you (skipping rhythm getting louder)

Music Box tape

There was a princess long ago
Listen to this bouncy version of the song. Notice how the male and female voices alternate. Join in the off-beat claps in the last verse.

More ideas

▶ Tell any of the traditional stories involving princes and/or princesses, such as *The princess and the pea*, *The frog princess*, *Cinderella* and *Rapunzel*.

▶ Sing 'Bell horses' from *Knock at the door*.

▶ Sing 'Yankee doodle' from *This little puffin* . . .

▶ Read *Princess Primrose* by Vivian French (Walker, 1995).

▶ Read *The second princess* by Hiawyn Oram (Picture Lions, 1995).

Cross-curricular links

Language

▶ Make up some rhyming spells to go with numbers:

Spell number one,

Turn into a swan.

Spell number two,

Turn into a shoe.

▶ Sit in a circle round a big bowl or pan (cauldron) and ask the children, one at a time, to put a pretend ingredient into the pot. As they let go of the ingredient, the children say what it is. Before you start, decide what sort of a potion you are going to make. It could be disgusting, it could be sweet-smelling. Make the ingredients match the potion. A crunchy potion, for example, might include cornflakes, dry leaves, toe nails and pebbles. Stir it, smell it and pretend to taste it. Does it make you smack your lips or say 'yuck'?

▶ Turn the play corner into a tower. Use a large cardboard box, with the back cut away, and put something inside the tower to stand on. Make battlements, a flag and arrow slits. A blue piece of material round the base could be a moat. Use a table for the drawbridge. Provide cloaks, crowns, baggy knickerbockers, tights, long dresses and cardboard swords. Let princesses rescue princes and vica versa. Use broom handles for horses. Introduce a scaly monster (rocking horse) and/or a wicked fairy. Encourage the children to act out *Sleeping Beauty* or to make up their own stories. Gather an audience to watch.

Maths

▶ Cut a long cane or stick to make it the same height as the tower. Lay it on the floor and see how many beanbags or hands or feet are needed to match its length. Record your findings. Take the stick round the room and look for things that are taller/shorter than the tower.

▶ Look at steps in or near your room. Count them. How high is each step? Measure them using cubes. If practical and safe, use the steps for a game: ask the children, one at a time, to stand on (or put a toy on) the first step, the top step, the second step, and so on.

Science

▶ Some materials change when they are put together. Show the children some 'mixing magic'. What happens when you put sugar, yeast and warm water together? Mix paint powder with water. Drop some ink into water. Mix soil and water. Add water to a large spoonful of wallpaper paste. Compare the appearance, colour and texture before and after mixing.

▶ Some materials change when heated or cooled. Show the children some *hot* and *cold* magic. Make ice cubes. Put the cubes near a radiator. Make a clay ball and put it in the oven. Make biscuits. Melt a bar of chocolate and then put it in the fridge. Compare the appearance, colour and texture before and after heating/cooling.

Art and craft

▶ Make decorated crowns using bits of jewellery, buttons, glitter, tinsel and silver paper.

▶ Make cardboard swords. Paint the blades silver or gold. Decorate the handles.

▶ Make a large picture of the tower in the forest. Everyone can paint and cut out a tree. Make the tower out of a large cylinder. Cut out battlements. Add a flag or two. Make a prince, princess and wicked fairy out of toilet rolls. Add them to the picture in appropriate places. ●

Goldilocks and the three bears

traditional story with sound effects

Goldilocks walks in the woods and loses her way. She finds a cottage. It's empty. The occupants – three bears – are out collecting wood. Goldilocks explores the cottage. She tests the chairs (too high, too low, just right) but breaks the smallest. She tastes the breakfast porridge (too hot, too cold, just right) and eats up all the porridge in the small bowl. She goes upstairs and tries the beds (too hard, too soft, just right). She goes to sleep in the smallest.

The bears return and find evidence of an intruder: 'Who's been sitting in my chair?', 'Who's been eating my porridge?', 'Who's been sleeping in my bed?' On being discovered, Goldilocks jumps out of the window and runs away.

▶ Before telling the story of the three bears show and talk about three different-sized teddy bears: big, small and middle-sized. Ask the children to say 'big bear' in a loud, deep voice, 'little bear' in a quiet, high voice, and 'middle-sized bear' in a middle-sized voice. Hold up the bears one at a time. Can the children name them correctly using the right sort of voice?

▶ Tell the story of Goldilocks and the three bears. The summary above may be helpful. Encourage the children to join in with the bears' questions using the appropriate bears' voices.

Sound effects

▶ Use a glockenspiel for Goldilocks. Show her skipping through the woods, creeping upstairs and running away.

▶ Find an instrument for each of the three bears. Play loudly and slowly for Daddy Bear, quickly for Baby Bear and in between for Mummy Bear. Make each bear walk, and then run. Play the instruments at the same time to describe the bears walking through the woods.

▶ Find something (e.g. instruments, voices, odds and ends) to make the sound of a breaking chair and porridge being scraped out of a bowl.

▶ Use a xylophone or keyboard to describe the bears going upstairs. If possible, stand the instrument on one end so that the lowest (longest) bars are near the floor. Tap the bars one at a time from bottom to top. Ask the children to use their hands to mime going upstairs.

▶ The bears are angry with Goldilocks. Practise making growly vocal sounds. Experiment to find instrumental growly sounds (e.g. shakers, guiros, low notes on guitar strings). Put egg boxes and pieces of corrugated card and plastic out for the children to scrape and rub. Use bits of dowelling or pencils for scrapers.

One, two, three, Hair - y bears I see. One is big, one is small, One is in - be - tween.

One two three

action song with simple instrumental accompaniment

One two three,
Hairy bears I see,
One is big, one is small,
One is in between.

One two three
Wooden chairs I see.
One is strong, one is weak,
One is in between.

One two three
Porridge bowls I see.
One is hot, one is cold,
One is in between.

One two three
Cosy beds I see.
One is hard, one is soft,
One is in between.

▶ Learn the song and add actions for lines three and four. The tune is similar to 'Baa baa black sheep'.

▶ Clap (tap, shake or scrape) three times on 'One two three'.

▶ Play a repeated note C on chimes, glockenspiel or xylophone throughout. Let the children choose when to play.

Teddy bear, teddy bear

action rhyme

Teddy bear, teddy bear, touch the ground,
Teddy bear, teddy bear, turn around,
Teddy bear, teddy bear, touch your nose,
Teddy bear, teddy bear, touch your toes.

▶ Chant the rhyme and add actions.

Musical teddy bears

game with instruments

Put an instrument in front of each child. Tell them to play only when instructed. For example, when they hear 'Teddy bear, Teddy bear, shake your tambourine', children with tambourines pick up their instruments and shake them. The leader mimes the shaking action for about five seconds and then stops. The tambourine teddies also stop and carefully and quietly put down their instruments.

▶ Change the instrument each time (e.g. 'tap your woodblock', 'beat your drum', 'scrape your guiro', 'jingle your bells').

▶ As the children become skilled at identifying instruments and playing them in a controlled way, give more specific instructions. For example: 'Shake your maracas quietly' or 'Rub your sandpaper blocks quickly.'

▶ The children can play this game in pairs in the music corner. One child gives the instructions and the other, the teddy bear, finds the instrument and plays. Swap over after a few goes.

Go to sleep Mr(s) Bear

game using loud and quiet sounds

Go to sleep Mr(s) Bear,
Go to sleep Mr(s) Bear,
We're going to hide your honey.

WAKE UP MR(S) BEAR!
WAKE UP MR(S) BEAR!
GO AND FIND YOUR HONEY.

▶ This game practises quiet and loud chanting and playing. One child, the bear, curls up in a pretend cave and goes to sleep. Everyone whispers the first three lines over and over again while someone hides the honey pot. Then everyone shouts the last three lines to wake the bear up. On waking, the bear walks around hunting for the honey pot. The observers clap quietly if the bear is a long way away from the honey. The clapping gets louder as the bear approaches the pot. Instead of clapping, use jingles or shakers to direct the bear.

Music Box tape

listening and joining in

Five big teddies

This simple song is sung to the tune of 'Ten green bottles'. Join in with the singing. Act it out. Listen out for the descending slide on the swanee whistle followed by a click on a woodblock as the teddies bite the dust!

More ideas

▶ Sing 'The bear went over the mountain' from *Apusskidu*.

▶ Sing/chant *We're going on a bear hunt* by Michael Rosen and Helen Oxenbury (Walker, 1993). Add actions and sound effects.

▶ Read and make sound effects for the story *Peace at last* by Jill Murphy (Macmillan, 1995) – see **Bedtime**.

▶ Have a teddy bears' picnic with honey sandwiches and games.

Cross-curricular links

Language

▶ Make up rhyming couplets about bears. Draw/paint pictures to go with them.

> I saw a bear
> Sitting on a chair.
>
> I saw a bear
> Eating a pear.

▶ Put out a selection of furry/hairy things (e.g. fabric, soft toys, wigs, bulrushes, sheepskin rug, clothes). Feel them and talk about them. Make a collection of describing words and phrases (e.g. soft, furry, like my rabbit).

▶ Make up a different ending to the story of Goldilocks and the three bears. It can be happy, sad, exciting or funny.

Maths

▶ Make the home corner into the bears' cottage, with teddy bears, chairs, bowls, spoons and beds in three different sizes. Talk about them using mathematical vocabulary of comparison.

▶ Use the things in the house to develop the children's understanding of relative size. For example: 'Put the smallest teddy in the largest chair' or 'Give Daddy Bear the biggest spoon'.

Science

▶ Talk about bears. Where do they live? How do they move? What do they eat? Do they all look the same? What are baby bears called? Are they tame?

▶ Talk about honey and bees. If possible, look at real (dead) bees and taste a honeycomb (check for allergies first). Feel and smell beeswax candles. Light them and see what happens to the wax. Look at, smell and use beeswax polish.

Art and craft

▶ Draw round three children: one tall, one small, one middle-sized. Fill in the
outlines using scraps of fur fabric and make them into bears. Add details
(e.g. ears, nose, eyes).

Drama

▶ Pretend to be Goldilocks skipping through the woods. Some children can be
trees. Swap over.

▶ Walk like Daddy Bear – slowly and with long steps. Walk like Mummy Bear –
roly-poly. Walk like Baby Bear – small steps, stopping and starting. Get into
threes and pretend to be the family of bears out for a walk. Talk to each other
in appropriately pitched voices.

▶ Pretend to be Goldilocks entering the house, trying the chairs, tasting the
porridge, going upstairs and going to sleep.

▶ Get into fours. Three children roar and growl while the fourth, Goldilocks, jumps
up and runs away.

▶ Use sounds practised earlier to accompany movements.

Cookery

▶ Make porridge and sweeten with honey. What happens to oats when they
are cooked?

▶ Make honey-flavoured flap-jacks.

▶ Have a teddy bears' picnic. Make cold drinks and honey sandwiches. ●

The ugly duckling
story with sound effects

Mother Duck sighed. She wanted so much to get off her nest and stretch her legs and feet, but the last egg would not hatch. The rest of the ducklings were dodging in and out of the rushes, peeping with excitement.

'Come on,' she muttered, nudging the egg with her bill. 'Get a move on.'

Some time later she felt a tapping beneath her. 'At last,' she said. 'And about time too!'

When the duckling finally got free of its shell, Mother Duck nearly fell out of the nest with surprise. It was big, and, in her opinion, ugly. By the time the duckling was six weeks old it was huge. The other ducklings laughed at it.

'You can't swim very well, your feathers are tatty and you can't even quack,' they scoffed. 'Go away, you're not one of us.'

The young bird paddled off to the other side of the lake and hid in the reed bed. The sun sank in the sky. The frogs croaked out their love songs. That night the ugly duckling fell asleep wishing she had never been hatched.

The next day she was awakened by the steady flapping of big wings. She looked up. Six white swans flew low over the lake.

'If only,' the ugly duckling whispered to herself, 'if only I were as beautiful as those swans.'

Winter came. The edge of the lake froze over and the ugly duckling had a hard time finding enough food to eat. However, the reeds kept her warm, and she became friends with a water rat who lived in a hole in the bank.

Slowly the weather got warmer. Spring showers fell on the lake and pussy willow and catkins decorated the trees. The ugly duckling was a lot bigger now and she found it hard to hide away in the rushes. She was paddling along by the bank one day when she heard the swans flying over. She looked up and called out, 'Please stop and talk to me. I'm so lonely.'

The swans circled round the lake and landed on the water nearby. 'Come with us,' said one of them. 'A fine young swan like you shouldn't hide away in the reed bed.'

'Me, a swan?' said the young bird in amazement. 'Yes,' replied the biggest swan. 'You are a very fine swan indeed.'

The swan, for indeed she was a swan, looked down at her reflection in the water. A handsome white bird with a long neck and orange bill looked back at her.

'I am a swan. I really am a swan,' she whispered happily to herself, and she flapped her wings, paddled her feet along the top of the water and slowly rose into the sky with her new friends.

Sound effects

▶ Tell the story and talk about it. Ask the children to close their eyes and pretend they are there by the lakeside. What can they hear? Jog memories by retelling parts of the story: peeping ducklings, quacking ducks, lapping water, wind blowing through the reeds, splashes, croaking frogs, flapping wings, rain. Which sounds can be imitated by voices? Experiment with instruments. Flap magazines for the sound of beating wings.

▶ Describe the sounds. Peeps are high and fast. Croaks are low and rough. Experiment with glockenspiels to make the sound of rippling water. Combine the sound of rippling water with the sound of the wind. Add the sound of rain falling on the water. These sounds go on for a long time.

Sound picture

game putting sounds together

Make a large picture or frieze of the story. Include the mother duck, nest, ducklings, ugly duckling in the reeds, flying swans and frogs (see 'Art and craft'). Give each child a sound to make. You could have a group of peeping ducklings, several quacking ducks, some frogs and flying swans and a few children to make the sound of the breeze and the lapping water and rain. Ask them to make their sounds as you point to their part of the picture. As they become skilled at making the sounds, try putting two or more sounds together. If possible, display the picture near the ground so that the children can play this game by themselves.

Peeps and quacks

making patterns using two contrasting sounds

Use voices to imitate peeping ducklings and quacking ducks.

Now make patterns using the two sounds. For example, you could have lots of quiet peeps followed by three loud solo quacks. Repeat this until you have created an interesting pattern of sound. The pattern might look like this drawn on paper:

peep   peep
peep peep QUACK QUACK QUACK peep peep QUACK QUACK QUACK

▶ Do the same using these pairs of contrasting sound:
    wind and rain
    rippling water and splashes

▶ Make sound effects to match the pictures below. Copy each picture onto a large piece of card and display near instruments. Encourage combinations of voices, body sounds, instrumental sounds and other sounds.

wind

rain

splash

Little Tommy Tadpole

poem with actions

Little Tommy Tadpole began to weep and wail,
For little Tommy Tadpole had lost his little tail.
His mother didn't know him as he sat upon a log,
For little Tommy Tadpole had turned into a frog!

▶ Chant the poem a few times. Encourage the children to join in key words (e.g. 'tail' and 'frog') then key phrases (e.g. 'weep and wail', 'lost his little tail', 'sat upon a log' and 'turned into a frog'). Keep the pace slow. Get as many children as possible joining in with the whole poem. Get louder during the last line and jump into the air on 'frog'. At the end let everyone jump around like frogs, croaking 'rabbit rabbit rabbit . . .'

Five lit - tle speck-led frogs sat on a speck-led log, Catch-ing some most de - li - cious bugs, YUM YUM!

One jumped in - to the pool where it was nice and cool, Then there were four green speck-led frogs, GLUG GLUG!

Five little speckled frogs

game song

Five little freckled frogs sat on a speckled log,
Catching some most delicious bugs, YUM YUM!
One jumped into the pool where it was nice and cool,
Then there were four green freckled frogs, GLUG GLUG!

Four little freckled frogs . . .

Three little freckled frogs . . .

Two little freckled frogs . . .

One little freckled frog sat on a speckled log,
Catching some most delicious bugs, YUM YUM!
She/he jumped into the pool where it was nice and cool,
Then there were no green freckled frogs – Ahhhhhh!

▶ Sit in a circle, put a pretend log in the middle and choose five children to be
freckled frogs. Flick tongues in and out to catch flies. One at a time, at a given
signal, the frogs jump off the log and into the pond. The singers rub their
tummies on YUM YUM and gulp twice on GLUG GLUG. If you like, make a pause
in the singing and add a tambourine splash after 'One jumped into the pool'.

Splish splash

listening game

Ask the children to *hop* around the room like frogs to the sound of a
woodblock or tambour. After a while, tap twice on a tambourine. This is
the signal for the frogs to jump into the pond and *swim* around until the
hopping sound begins again.

Music Box tape

listening and joining in

Little green frog

Listen to the song and talk about it. The frog has no tail because it
doesn't need one. Which animals have tails and why? The frog has no
wings because it doesn't fly. Which animals have wings? How do frogs
get around? Talk about the strong back legs and webbed feet of frogs.
In the 'Ku-wak-wak-wak' chorus the children can swim quietly around
the room. Stop and listen as each new verse is sung.

More ideas

▶ Sing 'Five little ducks went swimming one day' from *Knock at the door*.

▶ Read *Tiddalik*: *the frog who caused a flood* by Robert Roennfeldt (Puffin, 1980). This is an adaptation of an Aboriginal dreamtime legend.

▶ Tell the traditional story of the Frog Prince.

▶ Sing 'There were six little frogs sitting on a well' from *Knock at the door*.

Cross-curricular links

Language

▶ Collect names of baby animals: cow/calf, cat/kitten, dog/puppy. Does anyone know what you call a baby swan?

▶ Frogs jump, tadpoles swim, swans fly. Describe the movements of other animals (e.g. snakes, panthers, dolphins, mice, kangaroos).

Maths

▶ In the song 'Five little speckled frogs' the numbers decrease as the animals either jump or swim away. Record using pictures and numbers. Older children can make up their own number stories and work out the answers using toys, cubes or children. For example: 'There were five frogs on a log. Two jumped in the water. How many were left?' or 'There was one duck swimming in the pond. Three more came along. How many now?'

▶ Play games matching frogs to lily pads, ducklings to eggs.

Science

▶ Draw a duck with the end of a wax candle – press hard. Add eyes, beak, feathers and feet. Paint all over the duck with a thin colour wash. Why doesn't the colour stick to the wax?

▶ Experiment with floating and sinking. Put out a variety of objects (e.g. wooden brick, ruler, apple, coin, marble, spoon, candle, bead, conker). Let the children take turns to put each object in a bucket of water to see if it will float.

Put things that float inside one hoop and things that sink in another. Label the hoops 'float' and 'sink'. Older children can record their results using drawings.

▶ Look after some frogspawn until it hatches into tadpoles. You will only need a small amount of spawn. Keep it in a tank not a bowl. Add weed and mud from a garden pond. Look carefully at the changes using a magnifying glass. Talk about the changes. Keep a tadpole diary. As soon as the tadpoles begin to change into froglets, return them to their natural habitat.

Art and craft

▶ Make frogs out of paper plates. Paint them green and brown and add stripes. Give them button eyes. Add legs – two short bent ones at the front, two long bent ones at the back. Make the frogs jump by flapping near them with newspaper. Have a frog race.

▶ Make frog headdresses and wear them for frog games.

▶ See how many shades of green you can make using just blue and yellow paint. Use the colours to paint frogs, trees, grass, apples and so on.

▶ Make a large picture or frieze of the ugly duckling's lake. Make the lake using horizontal strips of tissue paper (shades of blue and grey). Print the reeds using the sides of rulers. Cut up green plastic bags for weeds. Paint trees along the bank. Use fur fabric or wood shavings for the duckling's feathers and twigs for the nest. The swans can be made out of white felt, real feathers or white paper. Sponge print the sky and clouds. Use the frieze to create a sound picture (see page 85).

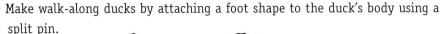

▶ Make walk-along ducks by attaching a foot shape to the duck's body using a split pin.

Drama

▶ Read the poem 'The tadpole'.

> **The tadpole**
> Underneath the water weeds
> Small and black I wriggle,
> And life is most surprising,
> Wiggle, waggle, wiggle.
> There's every now and then
> A most exciting change in me,
> I wonder, wiggle, waggle,
> What I shall turn out to be.
>
> *Elizabeth Gould*

▶ Make a wiggling sound using maracas, guiros or bells. Practise wriggling various parts of the body: head, tongue, fingers, toes, bottoms, knees. Start slowly and get faster. Let the music dictate the speed.

▶ Mime the life cycle of a frog. First ask all the children to make themselves into round shapes and then bunch together like frogspawn. Move gently on the spot. Begin to wiggle now and then. Wiggle a bit more, and wiggle away from the main group. Pretend to grow legs and swim to dry land at the edge of the room. Finally hop around the edge of the room, sometimes jumping into the pond for a swim. Find sounds for each stage of development and use them to direct the mime sequence. ●

The minibeast parade

song with actions and instrumental accompaniment

Pom, pom, pom, pom,
Pom, pom, pom, pom,
Pom, pom, pom, pom,
POM!

Wiggle like a worm,   *(echo: Wiggle like a worm)*
Wiggle like a worm,   *(echo: Wiggle like a worm)*
Wiggle like a worm   *(echo: Wiggle like a worm)*
In the minibeast parade. *(echo: In the minibeast parade.)*

Pom, pom, pom, pom,
Pom, pom, pom, pom,
Pom, pom, pom, pom,
POM!

Slide like a slug,   *(echo: Slide like a slug)*
Slide like a slug,   *(echo: Slide like a slug)*
Slide like a slug   *(echo: Slide like a slug)*
In the minibeast parade. *(echo: In the minibeast parade.)*

Flutter like a moth . . .
Bumble like a bee . . .
Scurry like an ant . . .
Crawl like a beetle . . .
Spin like a spider . . .

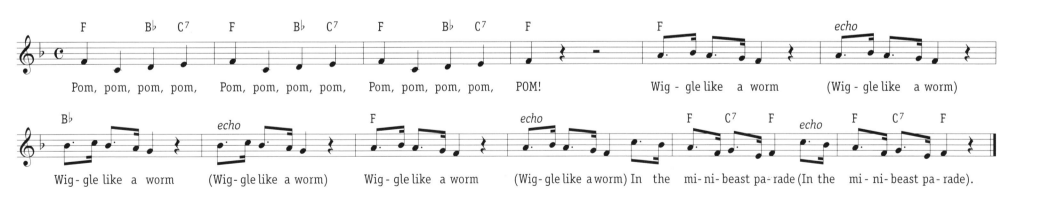

▶ Start off in a sitting position. Make up a hand/arm action for each minibeast and add to the echo lines. Tap thighs in time with the 'poms' in the chorus.

▶ Talk about some of the creatures mentioned in the song. How do they move: fast or slow; in a straight line or all over the place; forwards or sidewards; low down or high up? Which parts of the body do they use? Try sliding along the floor without using arms. Use arms as wings and fly around like moths. Crawl on feet and hands like beetles.

▶ Experiment with instruments to find sounds to match each minibeast. Accompany the echo lines with a short instrumental passage:

Wiggle like a worm,	*(shake maracas rapidly)*
Wiggle like a worm,	*(shake maracas rapidly)*
Wiggle like a worm	*(shake maracas rapidly)*
In the minibeast parade.	

▶ Make a picture card for each minibeast. Put the cards on the music table with a selection of instruments. Encourage the children to search for sounds to go with the pictures. Try putting two or more cards in a line and playing a sequence of sounds. You will need one child for each card/sound.

Minibeast rhymes

rhymes for quiet speaking, playing and scoring

Beetle
I saw a beetle
crawl – crawl – crawl
I saw a beetle
crawling up my wall.

▶ Sit on the floor in a line all facing the same way. Slowly and very lightly the children walk their fingers up the back of the person in front of them. Combine this activity with speaking. Aim to make the fingers move in time with the rhythm of the words.

▶ Accompany with very quiet scratchy sounds made with paper, toothbrushes, maracas, guiros or fingernails. Can you really hear beetles crawling?

▶ How would you draw the beetle's sound? You could show quietness by making the drawing small. Start low on the paper and move upwards. Get someone to move a finger or pointer along the score as the beetle sounds are made.

Garden snail
Slowly, slowly, very slowly
Creeps the garden snail,
Slowly, slowly, very slowly
On the wooden rail.

▶ As above, but this time use the whole hand to imitate the snail/slug movement. Keep fingertips still, slide the heel of the wrist up towards them, then lift up the fingertips and move them forwards a few centimetres.

▶ Accompany this movement with very quiet slurping mouth sounds, or with a continuous sound made by sliding palms over paper. Has anyone ever heard a snail moving?

▶ Draw the snail's progress. Can you show the humping movement? Make the line continuous. You will need a long thin piece of paper. Point to the score as you make the sound.

Ladybird

A ladybird came on my hand one day,
She stayed for a while – then flew away.

▶ Hold one hand out, palm upwards. Flutter the fingers on the other hand and let them land on the outstretched palm. Fly them away at the end.

▶ Experiment to find a wing sound by flapping small bits of paper (e.g. tissue paper, toilet paper, foil, writing paper, thin card). When each child has chosen his or her 'wings', combine the quiet flapping sounds with the words. Pause the sound for lines three and four.

▶ Draw the flight of the ladybird. Start high, land, pause, then fly off. How will you show the ladybird resting on the hand? Use the score to control the sound. When the pointer reaches the score where the ladybird rests on the hand, stop the flapping and observe a few seconds of silence.

Bee

What do you suppose?
A bee sat on my nose.
He said, 'I beg your pardon,
I thought you were the garden!'

▶ Use one hand to describe the fast and curving flight of a bee. Zoom around the face before landing on the nose. Fly off at the end and land on another part of the body or on the person next door.

▶ Experiment with voices and instruments to make a continuous buzzing sound. Buzz before and after the speaking. Make the buzzing louder as the bee approaches the nose, and fade it out as the bee departs.

▶ Draw the erratic flight of the bee. Find a way to show silence as the bee rests on the nose. Use the score in conjunction with the sound effects.

Minibeast chants

clapping and playing word rhythms

 Make some minibeast rhythm cards. Draw the creature on one side of the card and its name and rhythm on the other. Start with three minibeasts, one of each rhythm type such as bee-tle (two claps), but-ter-fly (three claps) and ca-ter-pil-lar (four claps). Make four cards for each creature, i.e. twelve cards in all.

▶ Start with the butterfly card. First identify the picture. Say 'butterfly' once, slowly. Tap out its rhythm on your thigh as you speak. Ask the children to count the taps. Show the children the other side of the card. Tell them that each black note head means one clap. Ask the children to tap and chant 'butterfly'. Point to the notes as they chant.

▶ Place four butterfly cards in a row with the rhythm side showing. Tap and chant four times.

 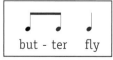 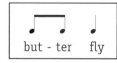 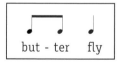

▶ Choose a child to accompany the chanting with a tambourine, tambor or claves.

▶ Take away two cards and ask a child to tap and chant or play and chant the 'music'. Help the children to understand that they must 'read' the music to get it right. Try with three cards.

Another time go through the same process with the two-clap 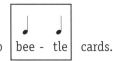 bee - tle cards.

Finally, introduce the four-clap 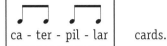 ca - ter - pil - lar cards.

Older children can try to chant and play minibeast combinations. To start with only put two minibeasts together, such as butterfly and caterpillar:

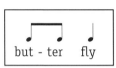 but - ter   fly    ca - ter - pil - lar

Increase to three then four. Experiment with repetition (e.g. beetle beetle caterpillar beetle).

Encourage the children to copy their minibeast rhythms onto paper.

Here are some more rhythms for you to try:

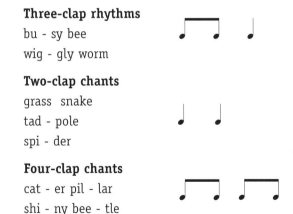

Three-clap rhythms

bu - sy bee

wig - gly worm

Two-clap chants

grass snake

tad - pole

spi - der

Four-clap chants

cat - er pil - lar

shi - ny bee - tle

Music Box tape

listening and joining in

Nine caterpillars

Listen to the song and join in the counting. Choose nine children to be the caterpillars and ask them to munch and smile during the verses and crawl around in the counting chorus. Experiment with instruments and other sound-makers to find munching sounds.

More ideas

There is a section on smaller animals in *Knock at the door*. You will find old favourites such as 'Little Arabella Miller', 'I wish I was a little grub' and the counting rhyme 'Here is the beehive'. There are also three lovely songs: 'One two three white butterflies I see', 'Fiddle-dee-dee' and 'There's a worm at the bottom of my garden'.

Cross-curricular links

Language

Help each child to make a minibeast (see 'Art and craft'). Make up an alliterative name for each one (e.g. Spooky Spider, Wezi Worm, Cedric Centipede, Barbara Beetle, Slimy Slug). Encourage the children to talk about their creature. How did they make it? What does it look like? What do they like about it? If it could speak, what would it sound like? Make up very short stories. For example: 'One day Wezi Worm was wriggling in the potato patch when a seagull swooped down and ate him.'

Maths

Play 'Legs', a game for two to four children. Give each child a legless beetle card (see page 93). The dots at the side indicate the position of the legs. The children shake a die and draw the corresponding number of legs on their beetle. When everyone has had one go, look at the beetles and talk about them. Have any of the beetles got all their legs? Which beetle has most/least legs?

Have any beetles got the same number of legs? How many legs are missing? Shake again and repeat the discussion until all the beetles have their full compliment of legs. You don't have to shake the exact number to finish. If you like, draw spare legs at the side.

▶ Play 'Legs' with spider cards – eight legs.

▶ Make some worms by cutting the legs off tights and stuffing them with paper or material scraps. Use a variety of tights (e.g. children's, adult's, opaque, see-through, plain, patterned, flesh-coloured, coloured). Which is the shortest/longest? Compare sizes by laying them next to one another. Measure with feet, bricks, hand-spans and so on. Which is the fattest/thinnest?

▶ Make a study of legs. Cut out pictures of people, four-legged animals, two-legged birds, spiders and insects. You could include centipedes. Put them in sets according to the number of legs.

2 legs

4 legs

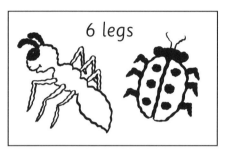

6 legs

Science

▶ Keep an eye open for minibeasts in the school environment. Look at them under a magnifying lens. Take care not to hurt them. Look at colour, pattern, texture, shape and size. Look for and identify joints and segments, legs, wings, eyes, antennae and mouths. How do the creatures move and eat? Keep a pictorial or written record of where the minibeasts were seen.

Siresh saw a spider in a dark corner.

Art and craft

Use a range of techniques and materials to make minibeasts – one per child, if possible. Here are some ideas.

SPIDERS

Attach eight legs (e.g. pipe cleaners, bits of string) to a stuffed and painted paper bag or large round plastic pot. Glue bits of wool or wood shavings onto the body to create a hairy texture. Add felt or button eyes. Suspend.

LADYBIRDS

Paint large flat pebbles with red paint. Add black spots later. Mix some white glue into the paint to prevent flaking and to give a gloss effect. Stick felt underneath and use as paperweights.

CATERPILLARS

Same as worms (see 'Maths') but put rubber bands round the body at several points to create segments. Add felt eyes and legs.

BEES

Glue together two yoghurt pots and paint with a black paint/glue mixture. When dry stick bands of yellow round the body with felt or crepe paper. Add wings made out of thin white card. Pencil in veins. Make dangly legs out of wire or string.

BUTTERFLIES

Same as bees, but with tubes for bodies, larger decorated wings and longer dangly legs. Use pipe cleaners for antennae.

SNAKES

Make bodies out of clay or plasticine. Make patterns and textures using old pencils, combs and lolly sticks. Paint and varnish the clay.

ANTS

Use a lump of brown plasticine for the body. Make legs out of twigs or brown pipe cleaners

SLUGS

Stuff dark socks with paper or material scraps. Put a ball of plasticine in the toe of the sock for the head. Stick black painted pipe cleaners or sticks into the head for antennae. Attach a strip of silver paper to the rear end for the tail.

SNAILS

As for slugs, but use a round painted plastic tub for the shell. Cut the tub to fit over the sock.

Make a garden for the minibeasts. Paint cardboard to make clumps of free-standing grass. Make a background of huge painted flowers. Stick petals on paper plates and attach the flowers to canes or long tubes. Add leaves. Suspend the flying insects. Put worms and snakes on the ground and ladybirds on the leaves. ●

BOOKLIST

Jan Betts, *Knock at the door* (Ward Lock Educational, 1980)

Veronica Clark, *High low dolly pepper* (A & C Black, 1991)

Veronica Clark, *Music through topics* (Cambridge University Press, 1990)

Beatrice Harrop, *Apusskidu* (A & C Black, 1975)

Beatrice Harrop, *Okki-tokki-unga* (A & C Black, 1983)

Elizabeth Matterson, *This little puffin . . .* (Puffin, 1991)

ACKNOWLEDGEMENTS

Acknowledgement is due to the following, whose permission is required for multiple reproduction:
A & C BLACK for words by Sue Nicholls to the song 'Spaceship to the moon'; A & C BLACK for words by Veronica Clark to the song 'Noah'; CAMBRIDGE UNIVERSITY PRESS for words and music by Veronica Clark to the song 'Five warm eggs in an incubator', taken from *Music through topics*; EVANS BROTHERS (AN IMPRINT OF HARPERCOLLINS PUBLISHERS LTD) for the poems 'In the mirror' by Elizabeth Fleming and 'The tadpole' by Elizabeth Gould; BARBARA IRESON for the poem 'Five little owls'; WARD LOCK EDUCATIONAL LTD for use of the poem 'My eyes can see' by Jan Betts from *Knock at the door*; WARD LOCK EDUCATIONAL LTD for words and music to the songs 'Trees' and 'All by myself' by Jan Betts; A.P. WATT LTD for use of the stories *Peace at last* and *Whatever next?* by Jill Murphy, published by Macmillan; NICK WESTCOTT for music to the song 'Noah'.

Audio cassette
The songs on the *Music Box* audio cassette to accompany this book are taken from the BBC Radio series *Music Box*, produced by Kate Walker. The Executive Producer is Brian Scott-Hughes.

Illustrations © Zoe Figg 1995

The Publishers have made every attempt to trace the copyright holders, and in cases where they may have failed will be pleased to make the necessary arrangements at the first opportunity.

INDEX

Songs

All by myself	17
Five little speckled frogs	86
Five warm eggs in an incubator	61
Hey Jim a-long	12
Hush little baby	35
I can see my nose	11
I'm a little robot	26
Jingle bells	43
Little Rabbit Foo Foo	20
Noah	55
Oats and beans and barley grow	65
One two three	81
Polly put the kettle on	70
Spaceship to the moon	41
The minibeast parade	89
The wheels on the bus	49
There was a princess long ago	76
Trees	22
We're driving down to London	47

Stories

Goldilocks and the three bears	80
Jack and the beanstalk	64
Little Red Riding Hood	22
Peace at last	32
The elves and the shoemaker	16
The gingerbread man	68
The little red hen	59
The ugly duckling	84
Whatever next?	38

Poems

Five little astronauts	40
Five little owls	22
Funny the way different cars start	48
In the mirror	10
Little piggy-wig	14
Little robot	26
Little Tommy Tadpole	85
My eyes can see	10
Rice and tuna	71
The tadpole	88

Rhymes

Bubble bubble bubble	70
Diddle diddle dumpling	18
Hickety pickety my black hen	61
Humpty dumpty	61
I had a little cherry stone	65
Minibeast rhymes	90
Pitter patter	54
Rain rain go away	54
Ride a horse to town	78
Teddy bear, teddy bear	81